T0358400

.

Routledge Library Editions

LABOUR

ECONOMICS

Routledge Library Editions – Economics

LABOUR ECONOMICS AND
INDUSTRIAL RELATIONS
In 5 Volumes

LABOUR

P SARGANT FLORENCE

Routledge
Taylor & Francis Group

LONDON AND NEW YORK

First published in 1949

Reprinted in 2003 by
Routledge
2 Park Square, Milton Park, Abingdon, Oxon OX14 4RN

Transferred to Digital Printing 2007

Routledge is an imprint of the Taylor & Francis Group

All rights reserved. No part of this book may be reprinted or reproduced
or utilized in any form or by any electronic, mechanical,
or other means, now known or hereafter invented, including photocopying
and recording, or in any information storage or retrieval system, without
permission in writing from the publishers.

The publishers have made every effort to contact authors/copyright holders
of the works reprinted in *Routledge Library Editions – Economics*. This has
not been possible in every case, however, and we would welcome
correspondence from those individuals/companies we have been unable to
trace.

These reprints are taken from original copies of each book. In many cases
the condition of these originals is not perfect. The publisher has gone to
great lengths to ensure the quality of these reprints, but wishes to point
out that certain characteristics of the original copies will, of necessity, be
apparent in reprints thereof.

British Library Cataloguing in Publication Data
A CIP catalogue record for this book
is available from the British Library

Labour
ISBN 0-415-31381-3
ISBN 0-415-31379-1

Miniset: Labour Economics and Industrial Relations

Series: Routledge Library Editions – Economics

LABOUR

by

P. SARGANT FLORENCE, M.A. PH.D.

PROFESSOR OF COMMERCE AND DEAN
OF THE FACULTY OF COMMERCE AND
SOCIAL SCIENCE, UNIVERSITY OF
BIRMINGHAM.

Routledge
Taylor & Francis Group

LONDON AND NEW YORK

THIS VOLUME IS NUMBER 25

First Published   -   -   *March*, 1949
Reprinted   -   -   -   *February*, 1950

CONTENTS

PART ONE

LABOUR RESOURCES AND UTILIZATION

PART TWO

LABOUR IN EMPLOYMENT

Chapter   *Page*

PART THREE

UNEMPLOYMENT

PART FOUR

THE DIRECTION OF LABOUR POLICY

LIST OF TABLES

INTRODUCTION

THIS book deals mainly with facts and generalizations from facts, but links them by argument relevant to practical problems in western civilization to-day. These problems revolve round the efficient full employment of labour in a more or less free market system of economy. The argument is largely about the conditions (including comparative wages) underlying industrial efficiency and maximum production from various labour resources at least cost.

Setting out by estimating man-power, analysing the human factor and measuring labour efficiency, the book summarizes recent evidence on employment conditions making for or against efficiency, and on the incidence of unemployment.

Unemployment is an inefficient use of labour, and policies are indicated both for increasing efficiency in employment and for decreasing unemployment. The last two chapters discuss who is to implement and direct these policies in the light of past and of possible future progress. Under our present economic system, trade unions, the employers and the state all take part in industrial control and the argument thus links trades unions as well as unemployment with the central theme of efficiency. Many text-books exist (several are in the list on pp. 223-4) which deal separately with the trade union movement and unemployment, and this work omits their analysis in detail.

The author would like to acknowledge permission from the *Political Quarterly* to reprint passages in Chapter VIII, and also the kindness of the National Institute of Industrial Psychology in providing Table 15. He is also most grateful to Dr. W. Baldamus and Mr. James Langley for reading proofs and making valuable suggestions, to Miss Dorothy Diamond for compiling the index, to his wife, Lella Secor Florence, for reading and correcting the original manuscript, and to his son, Noel Florence, for information on modern piece-rate setting practice. Valuable advice was given at many points by colleagues at Birmingham, especially Professor Gilbert Walker.

9

PART 1

LABOUR RESOURCES AND UTILIZATION

CHAPTER I

MAN-POWER

§1 MAN-POWER AND ITS COMPOSITION

THE main issues discussed before 1939 under the title of Labour were unemployment or else trade unions. During and since the Second World War, however, problems have confronted the nation with issues closer to economic theory: the supply, the supply price and the efficiency of labour in face of an overwhelming demand for labour. The efficiency of labour in employment and the wages and other conditions to which the supply responds will, in view of recent neglect occupy in Part II a large portion of this book before proceeding to employment in Part III and to the labour policy of trade unions, employers and the State in Part IV. Basic to employment, unemployment, and policy are the total potential labour supply and analysis and measurement of the efficiency of its use—either as degrees of efficiency in employment, or as total inefficiency and waste out of employment. These are the issues to be discussed here in Part I.

The potential supply of man-power for labour is the total population less children and old people incapable of work. At the last census of population in 1931, as Table 1 shows, occupied men numbered over two-thirds of all males. If we subtract children of fourteen and under from the population, occupied males form 92 per cent of the remaining, adult, males (14,790 out of 15,992) and if we allow for students and retired old people, the occupied man-power is almost identical with the fit population. It is different in the case of women, since the

11

TABLE 1: MAN-POWER, 1931.

TOTAL OF 21,055 THOUSAND OCCUPIED IN GREAT BRITAIN,[1] ANALYSED BY SEX AND AGE, BY INDUSTRY AND BY STATUS.

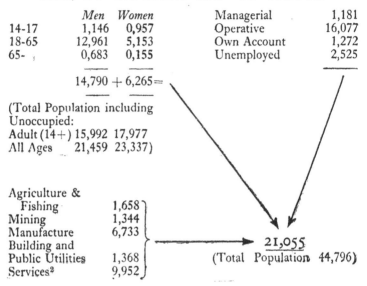

	Men	Women		
14-17	1,146	0,957	Managerial	1,181
18-65	12,961	5,153	Operative	16,077
65-	0,683	0,155	Own Account	1,272
			Unemployed	2,525

14,790 + 6,265 =

(Total Population including
Unoccupied:
Adult (14+) 15,992 17,977
All Ages 21,459 23,337)

Agriculture & Fishing	1,658
Mining	1,344
Manufacture	6,733
Building and Public Utilities	1,368
Services[2]	9,952

21,055
(Total Population 44,796)

bulk of adults are housewives, working—but not for pay, and therefore not technically "occupied."

Besides sex and age Table I presents two other ways into which the total occupied population of Great Britain must, for different practical purposes, be divided, namely by status, and by industry. The total from each of the three analyses adds up to the same 21,055,000 occupied, out of a total population of 44,796,000. Much can be learned from Table I, not only about the immediate past of Britain's economic structure but as a background for future discussion (including the use of words). Four points of fact and terminology must continuously be borne in mind.

[1]England and Wales, and Scotland (excluding students).
[2]Among whom defence 251,000 and private domestic service 1,626,000.

(i) The proportion of the population which is occupied will fall as the school-leaving age is raised. Owing to the fall in number of births in the last decade or two, the young will in future constitute a smaller proportion of the population, and the old constitute a larger proportion. Those at working ages, between the very young and the very old, are therefore, apart from school-leaving changes, likely to remain a constant proportion of the total population for some time to come, though the older half, aged over forty, will increase faster than the younger.[1] The proportion of the population which forms industrial man-power could be raised, however, by more women of working age going out to work (over a million left industry between June 1945 and June 1946) or by improving the health and working capacity of the old so that normal working life would be extended.

(ii) Nearly half the occupied population are in service industries and (apart from the armed services and indoor domestic servants) the proportion is increasing. This is partly due to the mechanization of production industries, partly to a rising standard of living which sets up a demand for personal services. The word "industry" will not be confined to production such as agriculture, mining, building and manufacture, but will include all occupied persons (usually excepting armed forces) grouped according to the process performed, the product made, the material used, or the service rendered to the consumer.

(iii) Not all the occupied population are actually at work as employees or operatives. The word "occupied" officially covers all persons *normally* employed for pay or gain, of whatever status, including those unemployed for the time being. It covers employers, managers, and those working on their own account (such as professional men or "small" shopkeepers).

(iv) Occupation has another more particular meaning. It refers to what a worker actually does within an industry. A man in some manufacturing industry may be engaged in actual production or repair; in transport, driving a lorry

[1]The detailed age distribution in industry in 1921-3 is given in Table 16, Chapter X.

belonging to the manufacturer; or in commercial, professional or domestic "occupations" like a clerk, an accountant or a cleaner. These occupations cut across industries. The same groups of occupations such as producers and repairmen, clerks or transport workers recur in different industries (including service industries); and among producer occupations the same grades such as skilled toolmakers or unskilled labourers also recur. Every group of occupation occurs to some extent in every industry, and we shall continually have occasion to refer to the criss-cross interlacing of occupation and industry.

§2 RECENT CHANGES IN MAN-POWER AND ITS ALLOCATION

The census of population is the only source from which the number of all persons working for pay can be recorded, whatever their status or age. In Britain this census, normally only taken every ten years, had to be omitted in 1941. To keep up to date on man-power, monthly estimates issued by the Ministry of Labour must, therefore, be used which include all occupied persons as in Table 1 except indoor domestic servants, men sixty-five and over and women sixty and over. In Table 2 the history of the mobilizing and allocation of man-power is traced by these estimates through pre-war, war and post-war years.

The total working population was apparently increased between 1939 and 1945 by almost 2,000,000, due partly to a rise in total population but mainly to an increase in the occupied women. Reduction of unemployment by over a million made the population actually at work (or in the armed forces) 3,000,000 more in 1945 than in 1939; but if armed forces are subtracted man-power in industry was less in 1945 than in 1939 by 2,000,000. The number of additional women enrolled in industry did not balance the number of men mobilized in the armed forces.

Recent changes in allocation of man-power are shown in Table 2. Man-power is divided first into armed forces, (including those on demobilization leave); then persons employed in industry manufacturing equipment and supplies for the forces, manufacturing for the home market, and for export;

TABLE 2: TOTAL AND ALLOCATION OF MAN-POWER IN GREAT BRITAIN 1939-48 MINISTRY OF LABOUR ESTIMATES, IN THOUSANDS

	Mid. 1939	Mid. 1945	March 1947	March 1948
Armed Forces[1]	480	5,130	1,506	1,123
Manufacturing:				
i. Manufacture for Forces	1,270	3,830	440	350
ii. Manufacture for Home Market ..	4,555	2,580	5,066	4,925
iii. Manufacture for Export	990	410	1,468	1,992
Basic industries and public services	4,763	5,318	5,674	5,842
Distribution and consumers' services ..	5,112	3,556	4,276	4,469
Building and Civil Engineering	1,310	722	1,210	1,355
Unemployed	1,270	103	560[2]	301
Total Working Population[3]	19,750	21,649	20,200	20,357

persons employed in basic industries and services (agriculture, fishing, mining, utilities, transport and government); persons employed in distribution and other services, and in building; and finally, the numbers unemployed. Each of these divisions show a characteristic man-power curve, before, during and after the war. The armed forces and the industries making arms naturally show a great bulge during the war. In 1945 they occupied 42 per cent of the working (and armed) population, as against 9 per cent in 1939. Basic industries are relatively stable and in fact have a gradual rise in man-power throughout 1939-47. The switch to the armed forces and industries making

[1] Including "not yet taken up employment."
[2] Fuel crisis.
[3] Less indoor domestic servants, men over sixty-five, women over sixty.

arms came therefore from manufacturers for export and the home market, and from distribution (and other services) and building. Here man-power at the end of the war was only 33 per cent as against 60 per cent in 1939 of total working and armed population. Since the war ended man-power has naturally shown a switch back, but the position in March 1947 still differed from mid-1939 in fewer unemployed, more in the armed forces (more than balancing loss to industry by unemployment), fewer in manufacture for armed forces, fewer in distribution and services, but more in manufacture both for the home market and for export.

Detail of the man-power in single industries can be brought up to date from 1931 only by reference to the workers insured against unemployment. Statistics were published before the war each year thanks to a count every July; since the war, numbers are given every month. These insured workers only include persons normally employed for wages in manual labour, or (if in non-manual labour) receiving less than £420 salary a year, and thus exclude employers and workers on own account. Insured workers also exclude those over 64 and indoor domestic servants. Before May 1936 agricultural workers and before September 1934 juveniles, fourteen to sixteen, were also excluded. Instead of the 21,055,000 occupied population in 1931, insured workers only numbered 12,500,000. For comparing the same industries or groups of industries between different years the record of insured workers will prove useful all the same. Among the basic industries, coal mining, for instance, is being urged to expand to meet post-war needs. Its insured workers were recorded at mid-1939 as 761,200, in mid-1945 as 717,600, in May 1947 as 734,800. Still larger falls in man-power (largely in fact woman-power) occurred between 1939 and 1947 in hosiery, textiles, clothing, footwear and furniture, though these industries were important for export, and made durable or semi-durable necessaries to replace war-time wastage.

Allocation of man-power between industries is clearly no less important than total man-power. For maximum efficiency new man-power must be found in the unemployed and the unoccupied (particularly women), and existing man-power distributed according to demand and need. This can be achieved by care in allocating new entrants into industry such as those long unemployed, the unoccupied and the school-leavers, or by mobility of labour between industries. With proper allocation of new entrants, and taking into account the criss-cross recurrence of the same occupation in different industries, relatively few workers need actually be switched from one occupation to another. Devices for securing voluntary mobility will be considered under wages and training.

§3 QUALITATIVE DIFFERENCES

The economist reckons man-power budgets in terms of units, assuming each man in a given occupation as of equal value; but it does not require psychologists to tell him that this assumption is at best a mere approximation. Individual persons in the same occupation differ in their capacity and willingness to work in that occupation, and those who have to grapple with labour problems must always bear these qualitative differences in mind. The existence of personal differences is common knowledge and needs no scientific elaboration; but the precise extent of the variation between persons, and the exact distribution of abilities at any job (or in the mental and physical ingredients needed for any job), is not common knowledge and must be further assessed by the help of psychology.

Measurements of people's heights have made us familiar not only with a range of variation between the short and the tall, but with the fact that the distribution of heights is such that there are more people at or around the average heights than at the extremes, and that the numbers taper off sym-metrically towards each extreme. In a given population we expect to find fewer dwarfs, say, at 4 ft. 6 in. or giants at 7 ft. than persons of medium height, say, at 5 ft. 9 in. The distribu-tion of heights follows, in fact, a normal curve similar mathe-matically to that of chance distribution. In his presidential address to the psychological section of the British Association in 1923, Sir Cyril Burt was able to announce that the distribu-tion of innate general intelligence also follows the normal curve. The abnormal and defective constituted no isolated types, but were simply the "tail end" of a chance distribution.

Moreover, the distance or range of variation between tail and head was great. In a survey of 30,000 London children it was found that within the elementary schools "the brightest child at the age of ten had the mental level of an average child of fifteen, while the dullest had the mental level of a little child of only five." Burt thought that all or most of our mental capacities were distributed in the same fashion. The normal distribution of the intelligence of children was confirmed by a testing of all Scottish children born in 1929 totalling 87,000. Adults who have been tested seem to be distributed very similarly in respect of general intelligence.[1]

Examination results and actual performance among groups of factory workers, taxi-cab drivers and coal-miners on the same job who were free from restriction of production, either mechanical or deliberate, also show a normal distribution often scattered over a wide range of marks or outputs.[2] The significance of this distribution is that in the first place a certain normal level of efficiency can be relied upon to which a majority will conform, a normal fair day's work can, for instance, be posited for any one job; but in the second place considerable deviations from norm are frequent—there is no dead level of equal intelligence.

The practical application of the distribution of human quality is complicated by variety in the quality of jobs. Some persons may be efficient at one job and not at others, some efficient in a wide variety of jobs, some not efficient at any jobs at all. In the first case vocational selection discussed in Chapter IX is particularly important; by its aid the square pegs can be fitted into the square holes, the round pegs into the round holes. But in the other two cases, the peg that will fit many holes and the peg that won't fit any, practical action is more difficult. Since general intelligence which varies so widely in distribution

[1] R. B. Cattell, *The Intelligence of Scottish Children*, Scottish Council for Research in Education. "Occupational Norms of Intelligence and the Standardization of an Intelligence Test," *British Journal of Psychology*, July 1934.

[2] Florence, *Statistical Methods in Economics and Political Science* pp. 69-70, 258-60.

Viteles, *Industrial Psychology*, Chap. VII and especially pp. 58-60.

Crofts and Caradoc-Jones, *Secondary School Examination Statistics*.

is an ingredient of ability to perform most (though not necessarily all) industrial jobs, both these cases are likely to be frequent; a generally intelligent worker will be fit for many kinds of job, a generally unintelligent worker for few, if any. National efficiency requires that the generally unintelligent should move into that job in which he will do least damage (below a certain level of intelligence unemployment may be indicated in the national though not necessarily the personal interest); and requires that the generally intelligent should move into the particular job of the many he can do where general intelligence is in greatest national need or demand. Testing persons already in jobs where intelligence is of varying importance, it is found[1] that though the average for each job comes out as might be logically expected (schoolmasters and students test on average higher in intelligence than clerks, clerks higher than skilled workers or shopkeepers and assistants, and all of these higher than unskilled labour) there is much overlapping. Some labourers test higher in general intelligence than some schoolmasters.

Obvious possibilities are thus presented for increasing national efficiency through greater mobility of persons between occupations. Re-classification cannot easily be performed at middle age when experience has already conditioned persons' reactions, and techniques proper to one occupation have already been learned and become difficult to unlearn. Opportunities must be thrown open early in life and mainly through the educational ladder. In England where the type of "public school" or secondary education and the chance of getting higher education still depends so greatly on the ability of parents to pay fees, the educational system has been shown to close doors to a large proportion of the able but poor. This misdirection and wastage of talent costs a nation dear in the level of efficiency of its industrial leaders and organizers.[2] Labour has to work under conditions less propitious than if industrial management and advice were in the ablest hands the nation could provide.

[1]Himmelwert and Whitfield, *British Journal of Industrial Medicine*, October 1944.

[2]*See* Gray and Moshinsky, and Glass and Gray, Chapters VIII, IX and X of *Political Arithmetic*, Ed. Hogben; and Florence, *Logic of Industrial Organization*, Chapter VIII.

CHAPTER II

THE HUMAN FACTOR AND THE ECONOMIC SYSTEM

§1 THE HUMAN FACTOR

THE "human factor" is a phrase much used in discussion to-day and it is for several reasons convenient to our purposes. The phrase supplements the fact of man-power given in the first chapter, and applies only after the number and kind of workers is determined. The "human factor'" could not be said to be increased by the mere addition of more men, and refers essentially to variations in efficiency *per man*. Once the total man-power is known, the question now is, how can the power of *each* man be increased?

"Factor," moreover, indicates that the state or behaviour of a given number of human beings is only one of the causes underlying the facts discussed. The word allows for several causes being at work which is nearly always the case in modern industry with its complex of "factors" human, economic and technical. Most industrial accidents, for instance, are due to a combination of human and material factors. A worker makes a slight slip which only becomes serious because he is physically in the midst of potentially dangerous equipment. The unemployment again of a particular person may be due to the human factor, perhaps to his temperamental make-up; but the fact that 10 per cent of all workers are unemployed at some given time and place is due to economic, rather than to human factors.

Finally the adjective "human" indicates that studies must not be based on some abstraction like economic man, but on man "in the round" with all the feelings, attitudes, sentiments, and behaviour that can be objectively observed, and interpreted as a result of observation. This is not a text-book of physiology or psychology and will deal primarily with outward behaviour associated with outward conditions. Nevertheless these associations between outward facts may often have to be traced through inward events. A regularly recurring fall in output may be observed at the end of a long working spell or day. Both fall in output and the number of hours worked are facts external to the human worker; but the explanation of the association between the two is usually "fatigue" internal to the human being, and by fatigue is usually meant both a physiological bodily occurrence, and a psychological element such as a feeling of tiredness. These three "concomitant" levels are normally involved in the employment of the human factor: external facts, like outputs; states of mind or attitudes, like morale; and states of body. Again, unemployment involves the external facts that human resources are wasted, output which might have satisfied wants is not produced, and a worker and family are short of normal income, poverty-stricken and becoming cumulatively incapable of work. The economist usually rested his case against unemployment there. Recently, however, the psychological concomitants have been realized such as demoralization, feelings of frustration and inferiority, and ultimate resignation to fate[1] and to perhaps permanent unemployability.

On the other hand there has been a tendency in American psychology, sociology and schools of social work to concentrate on the mental attitude both of the employed and the unemployed worker quite apart from the consumer's need or demand for his work. This is economic abstraction in reverse. A manual on labour must not neglect what labour is ultimately *for*, and in this book the consumer's demands and needs which an economic system tries to satisfy will be kept in view, as well as the satisfaction of the producer's "human nature."

§2 HUMAN NATURE AND ECONOMIC FORCES

An economic system is part of the attempt to meet the needs of human beings from the natural and human resources at their disposal. In most sectors of the present system human needs are measured by demands on the market at various prices, human resources by the supply of labour and management

[1] M. Jahoda, *Die Arbeitslosen von Marienthal*. Archbishop of York's Committee, 1938; *Men Without Work*.

offered at various wage and salary rates. Chapter I analysed the total supply of labour actual and potential; here we have to discuss how potential supplies may become actual, that is, how workers may be got to exchange their services for terms compatible with demand—with the prices that consumers offer. The problem falls conveniently and conventionally into two parts considered in Parts II and III of this book. There is the problem of the inefficient employment of labour, and the problem of no employment at all—of unemployment. Unemployment may be defined as the idleness of the willing and capable. It assumes that labour is willing and able to work (though not necessarily to move), but that the demands of public and private consumers and investors are not sufficient to employ the supplies of labour, however capable and willing.

Inefficient employment of labour on the other hand is largely a failure to obtain the full willingness and capacity of labour. Full demand is not met, because all labour employed is not stimulated to produce adequately, and some labour not stimulated to move where work is required. Unemployment and industrial inefficiency, though conventionally considered separately and usually by separate authorities in separate books, nevertheless interlock at many points, and have common factors. Both are wasteful of national resources with their wastes capable of being measured as described in Chapter III; both can be prevented or controlled by social policy as set forth in later chapters, and each acts and reacts on the other. Fear of unemployment for oneself or for mates will slow down willingness to produce, or to move between industries and districts; unemployment itself will cause inefficiency in future employment by reducing income and lowering nutrition and working capacity. On the other hand, fear of unemployment has proved an incentive reducing labour turnover and absence —an incentive which the guarantee of full employment may remove. Unemployment, again, in eliminating wages and reducing income to benefit level has been considered a stimulus for workers to move on to other industries where products and services are in greater demand; before benefit was paid, it was a drastic "repulsive" from industries and occupations where the demand of the community did not want all the existing labour supply.

The state of mind and body induced by unemployment can thus be studied along the same lines as that of ineffective employment. An unemployed worker's feelings of frustration and his cumulative loss of efficiency can be paralleled by the feelings of boredom (and probable inefficiency) of workers employed in jobs unsuitable to their capacities. The causes of unemployment and inefficient employment are also inter-related. If a worker is below normal in his capacity or willingness for work and thus less efficient in a given job, or if he is below normal in his capacity and willingness to move to jobs in greater demand, the chances of his being employed at the normal wage are clearly diminished. Thus lower rates of unemployment could undoubtedly be reached if steps were taken to strengthen incentives to work efficiently and attractives to move where work was offered, or to increase capacity for work of various kinds.

Modern economists have not on the whole spent much time on the efficiency of labour as an element in unemployment. With the high rates of unemployment prevailing between 1920 and 1939, the supply of labour was certainly a less likely place to look for remedies than the demand for labour. With the inauguration of Government policies of full or at least high and stable employment, however, plans to improve the efficiency of the labour supply will have to be carefully worked out. If we accept the evidence given in Chapter I, human nature is differentiated and variable in capacity and when the rates of unemployment get as low as, say, 3 per cent of the numbers insured it may well be the relatively incapable who are out of work. A certain proportion may be incapable of doing the kind of jobs required anywhere, and a further proportion of doing the kind of jobs offered where they live, and yet unwilling or unable to move elsewhere. Though it may satisfy the worker to be employed when and where he likes, the cost to the consumer may be too high. There must be some kind of harnessing and unharnessing of workers in accordance with community needs, and methods of stimulating work when and where it is required most.

§3 THE HUMAN FACTOR IN EMPLOYMENT

What facts will determine whether a man or woman takes to work that is wanted and works efficiently? A wide view must include three categories of fact: the person's own nature, whether he or she is capable and willing, intelligent and strong, energetic or lazy; the traditional social pattern, for instance, whether married women are allowed by convention to work away from home; and finally any stimulus that may be applied. Differences in intelligence and temperament were touched upon in the first chapter and will be further discussed in Chapter IX, and the force of social conventions will be often referred to in later chapters, particularly VI. The facts of both categories, however, are not easily changed; and it is the effects of various stimuli that will be of chief interest in this book. The main alternative stimuli are coercion and inducement. Coercion in "directing" labour into war industries and keeping it there was used in Britain by the Government during both world wars. But in peacetime a "free" society does not normally rely for needed work in industry, or movement to needed work, on the physical coercion of the individual, and a stimulus must be offered to the worker's willingness where social conventions and attitudes or his own nature make him unwilling.

Whether coercion or inducement is used, an effective stimulus must include increasing the *capacity* of the worker to work or move. Willingness and capacity are states of mind and body that shade off into one another as is admitted in popular slang by a regular spectrum of colours (the latest is "browned off") which includes gradations of fatigue and unrest:

At one pole is yellow, the symbol of hatred and ill-will; at the other pole red, the danger signal of physiological breakdown and absolute incapacity. Green is the symbol of envy, and also of a lack of self-reliance and a mental instability and restiveness often found in the raw "greenhorn" not at home in his environment. Blue is the symbol, not to say symptom, of a slightly more physiological malaise and despondency, a state of low stimulation midway between positive ill-will and positive ill-health.[1]

For practical purposes, however, capacity (largely physiolo-

[1]*Florence, Economics of Fatigue and Unrest*, p. 384.

gical) and willingness (largely psychological) may be distinguished as the two basic elements that can be stimulated in the human factor. The impact of a free economic system on labour can thus be pictured as four processes:

$$
\text{Stimulus} \begin{cases} \text{To capacity} & \begin{cases} \text{To work (i)} \\ \text{To move (ii)} \end{cases} \\[2ex] \text{To willingness} & \begin{cases} \text{To work (iii)} \\ \text{(incentives)} \\ \text{(To move (iv)} \\ \text{(attractives)} \end{cases} \\ \text{(inducement)} \end{cases}
$$

Words should be found to indicate each of these four processes. Stimuli to the will to work already have a name in common use—"incentives"; and stimuli to the will to move to particular jobs that need doing may obviously be called "attractives." The opposite of incentives and attractives may be known as "deterrents" and "repulsives." An incentive or attractive may for short be called a nexus. The cash-nexus is the wage or other financial consideration which binds a man to his job, but as will be seen there are many non-financial attractives and incentives. A man may find an incentive or attractive in the love of the job, or by the honour involved, or by a sense of duty, or even in the incidental sport of the thing; when a hobby, fame, duty or sport nexus may be said to exist. But language halts behind thought when it comes to the stimuli to the workers' capacity. When capacity is stimulated by additional food—higher wages is often a simple expedient—the word nutritive may be applied, but this does not cover the process whereby working capacity is stimulated by changed physical conditions at the place of work or elimination of fatigue by shortening hours. We can speak of an enabling or disabling effect but for a simple word we must fall back on "conducive." A condition may be called "conducive" to efficiency in a given job if it increases a worker's capacity for working or moving; or to put it differently, if it facilitates incentives and attractives.

The relation of the economic system and human nature is the basic problem of labour, and economists, psychologists and physiologists have all surveyed parts of the ground from different points of view. Psychologists have taken up incentives; physiologists paid attention in the First World War to the disabling effects of long hours of work and certain physical conditions and recently to nutrition. Neither psychology nor

TABLE 3: CHART OF INFLUENCE OF EMPLOY-MENT CONDITIONS UPON EFFICIENCY THROUGH THE HUMAN FACTOR.

Terms and Conditions of Employment.

The Work-Place	The Wage	The Worker
H o u r s and speed-up of Work Chapter IV	Amount and M e t h o d of payment Chapters VII and VIII	Selection ᵗ of Individuals & T y p e s o f Worker Chapters IX and X
Type of Work Chapter V		
Physical Con-ditions Chapter V		Training Chapter IX §4
Social Rela-tionships Chapter VI		

HUMAN FACTOR
(Capacity & Willingness)

Quantity Quality and Economy of OUTPUT	ACCIDENTS	ABSENCE AND STRIKES	LABOUR TURNOVER (Mobility)

Measures of Efficiency

physiology, however, has given sufficient attention to the ways of attracting and mobilizing labour into particular jobs, if the economic system is to satisfy human needs and demands. A manual dealing with labour thus has a contribution to make, besides the study of unemployment and of labour organization, in tracing the connection of terms and conditions of employment with mobility between jobs as well as efficiency in a job. The complete picture of the inquiry into the conditions of efficiency in employment that forms the scope of Part II of this manual is given in Table 3.

§4 CONDITIONS OF HUMAN EFFICIENCY AND MOBILITY

The argument of Part II is based on the two simple propositions that variations in the human factor are largely due to variations in the conditions or terms of employment, and that variations in efficiency and mobility are largely due to variations in the human factor. These propositions are just another way of saying that the terms and conditions of employment stimulate efficiency or inefficiency, mobility or immobility through the intermediacy of the human factor. What precisely are these terms or conditions of employment? And first of all, what is employment?

When employed, persons are selected (and possibly trained) to carry out orders for a financial consideration under certain predetermined conditions. These conditions include certain hours of labour and physical and social conditions found at the place of work, and the orders relate to the performance of certain types of work at given speeds. Terms and conditions, therefore, include hours and speed of work, types of work, physical and social conditions of the workplace, wages and various methods of paying them and also methods of selecting and training workers. These are the terms and conditions occupying the top half of Table 3. On the left are the conditions pertaining to the work, in the middle are the terms pertaining to the financial consideration and on the right the conditions pertaining to the worker. Since workers are selected by classes (i.e., men skilled or unskilled, boys, women) and individually also, selection of the worker is a two-fold condition and training past or present a third condition of the worker.

The first proposition of the argument is indicated in Table 3 by the main and subsidiary arrows pointing from terms and conditions of employment to the human factor. Variations in conditions, for instance a reduction in hours of work, or a change in wage rates or in methods of selecting workers, will affect human capacity and willingness. The second proposition is illustrated by the lower half of the table. The human factor is depicted as affecting in its turn, by variations either in capacity or willingness, certain measures of efficiency and mobility. These measures (together with measures of unemployment) are taken up in detail in the next chapter, when one of the questions asked is precisely how far the human factor can be held responsible for accidents, loss in output and the other measures of efficiency.

The responsibility, we shall find, varies. Sometimes conditions will by-pass the human factor altogether as when an accident occurs purely for technical or mechanical reasons, or outputs rise with changes in material conditions such as speeded-up machines, or with altogether new types of equipment, without any reference to human intermediacy. This possibility must not be lost sight of in the scientific canvassing of the factors involved or in the practical treatment devised. Until recently, indeed, employers thought of no other factor than the material or mechanical. The plea of Robert Owen to his fellow employers over a hundred years ago is still relevant that "if the care which you bestow upon machinery can give you such excellent results, may you not expect equally good results from care spent on human beings, with their infinitely superior structure?"

Where the human factor *is* involved, some conditions and some measures of efficiency will mainly work through the channel of human willingness, others mainly through that of human capacity. Different social relationships or different methods of pay are likely to change the degree of willingness rather than of capacity to work and to be associated with voluntary restriction of output, absenteeism, strikes and labour turnover. On the other hand, the length of working hours and physical conditions are likely to affect health and capacity to work rather than willingness. A similar distinction is important in discussing mobility. Differences in the amount of wages paid in different industries is likely to make workers more *willing* to move from one to the other and thus perhaps to avoid unemployment. On the other hand, training workers in more than one trade or diversifying industry so that more than one trade is found in one place are conducives to the *capacity* of labour to move from one trade to another.

In seeking to reduce inefficiency, an effective change in conditions cannot be prescribed until it is known whether the human factor is the channel and, if so, whether it is mainly incapacity or unwillingness through which the condition is affecting efficiency. If a low output can be attributed to voluntary human restriction a remedy must be sought in new incentives, perhaps a new method of wage payment or new social relationships, not in conducives to greater capacity such as more healthy physical conditions. Similarly, if the problem is unemployment in a particular trade due to immobility it is a vital question, whether it is incapacity or unwillingness to move—a question which will be taken up in Part III.

The different sorts of employment conditions which may affect the human factor and ultimately industrial efficiency, are so variegated that there is practical and scientific value in making a list as in Table 3. Feelings of monotony for instance, which affect output and are so prevalent in modern industry must not be attributed to one condition solely. There is probably a multiplicity of causes at work and the seeker after truth (and a remedy) should canvass every type of condition given in the table. Is part of the cause long uninterrupted hours, a repetitive type of work, drab physical surroundings, dull society, time wage without targets, selection of intelligent workers to do purely routine work? All these conditions, as we shall see, are possible causes, either separately or in conjunction.

The scientific approach in studying efficiency of labour in employment is to correlate the conditions that might affect efficiency with measurable tests of efficiency. Each condition should be varied while the others are kept constant so as to isolate the factors, as in a laboratory. But though each of the conditions is studied in isolation, their mutual action and reaction must not be left out of sight. The effect of long hours is different, for instance, on different types of work; the effect of repetitive work monotonous to some workers, but not to others. In short, Table 3 serves as a guide to the experimental isolation of conditions, and also to the practical integration of conditions as a basis of policy.

§5 SUMMARY AND ARGUMENT

Once the potential and actual extent of man-power has been reviewed, man must be studied intensively in his relation to work. This relation is the subject matter of "labour," but the phrase "human factor" is useful because it indicates that efficiency is the result of a multiplicity of factors of which labour is one, and that labour is human and not just the abstraction which economists often make it. The opposite error must not, however, be made of considering labour in abstraction from the economic system. Here labour appears as a factor in supplying the demands of the consumer on certain terms of exchange, or if exchange is not effected, appears as unemployed. Students of unemployment have usually not been the same people as students of inefficiency in employment and there has been insufficient coordination and correlation of the two lines of study. Yet inefficiency, including immobility, and unemployment have some common causes and (as described in the next chapter) their industrial and social wastes and costs are capable of comparable measurement. Both may involve similar feelings of frustration and "browning off" and each may interact on one another.

Part II of this book will take in turn the various external objective terms and conditions of work such as hours of employment, wages, types of training and workers and show how each influences output, accidents, absence and labour turnover and other "industrial," objective measures of efficiency. These measures, as well as constituting tests of efficiency, have an importance of their own like the comparable measures of unemployment. Conditions of work influence them chiefly through the human factor which can be resolved into capacity or willingness to work or to move. Thus the methods of wage-payment can mainly be considered as an incentive (or stimulus to willingness) to work; differential wages (or lack of wages resulting from unemployment) as a stimulus to move; hours of employment mainly as affecting capacity to work; training as affecting capacity to move from job to job. The treatment of measures of inefficiency in employment and of unemployment in the next chapter, and of the effect of various conditions of work one by one in the following chapters, must not obscure their interconnections. Several conditions may be simultaneously at work causing inefficiency of various kinds. Adjustments of any one of them may offer alternative methods of avoiding inefficiency, or it may be necessary to adjust several conditions of employment together.

CHAPTER III

MEASURES OF LABOUR EFFICIENCY

§1 INEFFICIENCY AND ITS COSTS

INDUSTRIAL tests of labour efficiency, or more accurately, measurements of *in*efficiency in the human factor or the use of it, should satisfy three requirements. They should consist of data objectively measurable and actually measured; they should be attributable at least partly to the human factor as discussed in the last chapter; and they should involve costs to the employer, the worker or society which can to some extent be avoided by industry—there should be a preventable gap between actual total costs and the minimum unavoidable.

Six such tests will be used: output, its quantity, quality and economy; accidents; absence; strikes; labour turnover; and, finally, unemployment. The logical connection between these six industrial tests is simple. Industry consists physically of workplaces (like factories, mines, shops) to which workers are appointed and which they attend for the purpose of work with minimum waste. Inefficiency may therefore occur either as a failure in quantity or quality of work; or as a failure to work without excess of materials, breakage of tools or accidents; or as absence—a failure to attend; or as labour turnover—a failure to remain appointed to a workplace; or as unemployment—a failure to remain appointed to industry at all.

The essence of inefficiency is high cost for a given productivity[1]. Before discussing each test of inefficiency in detail, the main costs involved may be tabulated, distinguishing costs to the employer and to the worker. All these tests involve costs to the community in man-power or production per man and may necessitate State expenditure in hospitals and other services, or in insurance contributions or non-contributory financial assistance; and most of the tests involve costs both to employer and worker. But Table 4 shows one gap in the

[1]*See* Florence, *Logic of Industrial Organization*, p. 12.

TABLE 4: CHART OF LABOUR INEFFICIENCY

MAIN COSTS INVOLVED:

MEASURES OF INEFFICIENCY	To Employer	To Worker
Loss of Output:		
Quantity	Loss of sales	Loss in piece-earnings
Quality	Loss of sales and materials	Loss of earnings on spoiled pieces
Economy	Loss of materials, equipment, etc.	Losses to be made good out of earnings
Industrial Accidents:	Compensation claims Absence or labour turnover costs Damage to plant and organization	Physical pain Absence costs *or* permanent loss of earning power, total or partial
Absence:	Disruption of teamwork Overhead costs	Loss of time and piece-earnings
Labour Turnover:	Absence cost till worker replaced Cost of training replacements Loss of output, till trained	—
Unemployment:	—	Loss of earnings Loss of morale

costs to the employer, and another in the costs to the worker. The employer may suffer little cost by unemployment, and the worker little by labour turnover in itself. These gaps are significant because they mean that prevention of the inefficiency involved is probably not being tackled by the two parties. Hence arises the need of the community to back up the singly suffering party. In times of trade depression it is now generally agreed that the State should take measures to keep workers'

B

employment high and stable. But in times of boom, except war-time boom, there is as yet no agreement on measures to reduce the employers' costs from excessive labour turnover by workers who do not lose thereby.

§2 QUANTITY, QUALITY AND ECONOMY OF OUTPUT

Not all output is measurable either in quantity, quality or economy. Easiest to measure is repetition work when the same standard units are produced day in and day out by a number of workers. Quantity of output can then be compared in number of units; quality by proportion of units spoiled and rejected on inspection; economy by waste materials or broken tools per hundred units. As mass production and standardization develop, so will the measurability of the output.

But do differences and changes of output, however measurable, indicate differences and changes in the human factor? The evidence of growing mechanization has given rise to the notion that speed of production is more and more set automatically. To meet this implied criticism of the output test, a grouping of the operations actually performed at typical factories is required which will analyse them according to the part played by the human being in determining speed, quality and economy of production. Such a grouping including every operation and occupation at a large mechanized American brass factory is given in Table 8 (page 66). The outstanding features of the analysis are that 64 per cent of the workers in this "mechanized" factory were not on mechanized work; and that for the majority even of the machine-work, the workers controlled speed, e.g., on man-driven, man-steered and man-operated machines. The human factor thus plays an important part in determining output even in modern mechanized factories; variations in output may be due either to the capacity of the workers or (as in voluntary restriction of output) to the willingness of the workers. Voluntary restriction is sometimes denied, but evidence offered and discussed in Chapters V §1, VI §2, VII §2 and especially VIII §§1 and 3 points to times and places where the *tempo* of work was slower than capacity warranted.

Is the output test an accurate and scientific indication of efficiency and avoidable cost both to the employer and to the nation? Modern industry uses costly equipment and organization, hence a fall in the quantity of output means not only less goods and services, but a certain waste of machine and management capacity. It is an "overhead" as well as a "direct" cost. A lower economy or quality of output means, in addition, a waste of material, raw or, worse still, semi-manufactured. To the worker the costs of lower output will be lower earnings if he is paid by the piece. But he will lose by low quality of output only if wages are not paid on spoiled pieces. If the worker is not paid by piece but time, he will not lose directly from his lower output though there will always be the risk of dismissal and at least temporary unemployment.

How far the actual quality and economy of output produced involve excessive and avoidable costs is usually not difficult to ascertain, since spoilage and wastage should normally be recorded. But until standards of productivity per man are laid down for each type of job and of equipment, costs of unnecessarily low quantity of output are more difficult to assess. It must be left to comparisons of actual experience under comparable circumstances.

§3 INDUSTRIAL ACCIDENTS

Accidents are recorded publicly. Factory inspectors tabulate accidents in manufactures causing three days absence and, for a wider group of industries, there are the accounts of compensation cases. Accidents are compensated only if they involve more than three days absence from work, though many factories keep records of every accident, however slight, requiring first aid. The records are summarized in statistics of frequency rates, for instance the number of accidents per year per hundred persons or per 100,000 work-hours; and in statistics of severity rates, for instance, the work-days lost from accidents per hundred days or 1,000 work-hours.

Table 5 gives the frequency rates in 1938 for the seven large groups of industries included under the national Workmen's Compensation Acts, distinguishing fatal from merely absence-causing accidents. Accident-rates have changed but little. In the mines the number of annual accidents is shown to have been 20.5 per cent of the number employed. About one person in .

TABLE 5: ACCIDENTS GRANTED COMPENSATION GREAT BRITAIN, 1938

	Accidents causing more than 3 days' absence 1938	Fatal accidents	No. of persons employed	Non-fatal accidents in the year per 100 persons empl'd	Estimated days lost per year per person employed[1]
Shipping	8,654	285	156,706	5.7	2
Factories	217,599	718	5,985,493	3.7	1
Docks	10,672	74	111,655	9.7	3
Mines	162,094	983	796,382	20.5	6
Quarries	7,974	73	78,573	10.3	3
Constructional	12,945	84	275,743	4.7	1½
Railways	19,952	248	455,949	4.4	1½
Total	439,890	2,465	7,860,501	—	—

five has an accident each year. If a miner's working life is fifty years he must, statistically, expect ten of these serious accidents. Even in manufacturing, the group with annually 3·7 accidents per head, a worker must expect two serious accidents in his working life.

The accidents here recorded are only those involving injury to human beings, but it is often thought that under modern conditions the responsibility for accidents is the machine's rather than the human factor's. This is not correct. An accident is by definition an unusual occurrence, presumably caused by some unusual act or happening. Now, modern machines and mechanized equipment act far more regularly than human beings and it is found in analysing accidents that a mechanical defect was at fault only in a minority of cases. To quote the official Ministry of Labour *Gazette* (1940, p. 284)—"It has been estimated that of nearly 200,000 accidents each involving more than three days absence from work, reported in 1939 under the Factories Act, 1937, only one quarter can be referred to failures of plant or of technical precautions such as machine guarding; the remaining three-quarters were due to lack of

[1]See §4 for method of estimation and bearing on the rate of absence.

care on the part of individuals, whether the injured persons or others."

"Lack of care" is perhaps rather too narrow a conception. In the majority of cases, accidents follow some unusual action on the part of the worker. His unusual action may be classed as due to thoughtlessness, including negligence, "larking" (alleged to be frequent among boys) and want of judgment; as due to ignorance; due to inattention; or due to a slow reaction. Slow reaction is dangerous once the train of unusual events has started; inattention dangerous both in starting and reacting to events. Thus the human factor may enter twice into the causation of an accident: in starting the train of events as by thoughtlessness, ignorance or inattention; and in failing to avoid the event as, again, by inattention, or by a slow reaction. Accidents purely mechanical in generation, because started by unusual mechanical action and subsequently unavoidable are infrequent. The usual accident situation in modern factories (as on roads) is that *human beings act unusually and react slowly among the potentially dangerous conditions of the machine age.* Danger is always present, but man makes it threaten and doesn't see, or fails to escape, the threat.

The main cost of an accident to the worker, apart from the pain and shock involved, lies in loss of earnings due to absence from his work or from (partial or total) permanent disablement. To the employer it lies in disruption of organization and perhaps damage to plant at the time of the accident, in absence or labour turnover cost (described later) while the worker recovers or has to be replaced, and in the legal obligation (which may be insured against) of paying compensation. The total of payments for accident compensation amounted in Great Britain in 1938 to £731,000 for fatal cases, £5,609,000 for non-fatal cases. Can this serious burden of cost resulting from industrial accidents be avoided? If the main cause of accident lies with the human factor then the fundamental remedies lie in tackling the conditions which make that factor liable to cause accidents. Ignorance, for instance, can be overcome by training; and inattention, thoughtlessness and slow reaction may partly be caused by fatigue due to long hours or to a heavy type of work. If "larking" is really a peculiarity of young boys, care must be taken before employing boys in factory danger spots. These practical methods of cutting costs and inefficiency will be taken up in Part II.

§4. ABSENCE

Absence records (often including tardiness or late arrival at work) are kept by a growing number of industrial firms and the facts are usually summarized either as a percentage rate of the total time scheduled to be worked, or as so many days per working year. Since there are about 300 working days in the year every 1 per cent of (scheduled) time lost is roughly equal to three work days lost per year.[1] In comparing records, a "technical hitch" often arises because of differences in the total number of days a worker can be absent without showing cause before his name is taken off the books. True comparisons are not possible between firms till some particular practice becomes standardized. Possibly a week should be the limit after which workers giving no satisfactory reason, such as sickness, would normally be considered to have left and to be a case of "labour turnover," described later. Sickness and accident cases may, for book-keeping purposes, be struck off the factory absentee lists after twenty-six weeks (i.e., six months) absence, and then be added as disability cases to the labour turnover records. But such long-term disability cases still remain a cost for the community as absentees from industry generally. The disabled must in fact be debited in the national books much like the unemployed.

Absence is obviously an action of the human factor. But it is not so obvious that it is a serious cost to the employer. Wages do not normally have to be paid to the absentee and the loss of his output thus appears to be offset. This appearance is deceptive, however, for in modern industry the constant overhead costs of idle equipment and unused services of salaried staff are heavy. There is also disruption of teamwork, which may in assembly industries reduce the output by more than the absentee's normal contribution.

How far is this cost preventable by industry? To what

[1]With the five-day week and 250 working days in a year, 1 per cent of time lost equals two and a half working days lost per year.

extent is absence the result of sickness due either to the individual's susceptibility or to his home circumstances which industry cannot prevent?

Absence, for reasons of incapacity duly certified medically (including non-industrial accidents as well as ill-health) is recorded by some firms and, more comprehensively, in the national health insurance system. Insurance records have not, however, been comprehensively tabulated and published for England except for a sample of all industries (see Table 16, Chapter X) and for certain industries (see Table 9, Chapter V) like cotton-spinning and printing. The Scottish Department of Health published the national insurance records for Scotland annually between 1931-32 and 1939, not, however, distinguishing incapacity by sickness and by disability after 26 weeks. Available evidence from firms and from national insurance is thus fragmentary; but, during peacetime conditions, the fragments agree in general result. From Table 16, giving calendar days lost by sickness up to twenty-six weeks, it can be calculated that, taking into account the age distribution of the insured workers (given in columns 2, 4 and 6), the average working days per year lost by reason of sickness up to six months will be about five for men, six for single women and perhaps twelve for married women. This is confirmed by Smith and Leiper[1], who published a series of records from firms, mostly commercial, showing that sickness up to four weeks caused absence of about four working days per year among men, five or six among women, mostly unmarried. Sickness extending beyond four weeks, say up to twenty-six weeks, added one more day's absence on average.

The "basic" English insurance data (reproduced in Table 16) refer to the years 1921-23. A less detailed English inquiry for 1921 to 1927[2] and the Scottish data for 1931-9 indicate that claims for sickness and disability have risen since 1921 owing perhaps to greater familiarity with the insurance system, and a rising level of income, which makes it easier for workers to lose the difference between wages and benefits. For there is no doubt that poverty induces the reverse of malingering. A

[1]Industrial Health Research Board, Report 75.
[2]Report by the Government Actuary, Cmd. 3548, 1930.

worker, though ill, may not in the past have been able to afford loss of wages, consequent on absence. Thus the absence officially due to sickness may now be somewhat higher than the basic records show. Unfortunately, research has been backward in bringing the detailed basic data up to date, and they must still be quoted for the days unavoidably lost in manufacture and commerce. To judge from colliery records, miners' rates are certainly considerably higher. The days per year absent because of sickness seldom average less than nine for the coal-face workers, seven for other underground and six for surface workers.

Absence by reason of accidents can be estimated from Table 5, and the results are given in the last column. The rate of accidents varies far more widely than sickness as between industries. From 40 to 45 per cent of the absence cases are found to last less than two weeks, less than 4 per cent (including lump sum compensation cases) over twenty-six weeks; and the average duration or "severity" per case is possibly little more than four weeks, in addition to the three waiting days, say thirty working days. Where the accident frequency rate, as in factories, was 3.7 per cent, this means an average of 30×3.7 per cent or about one day lost by accident per man per year. In mining, where the duration per case was slightly longer, the accident frequency rate was 20.5 per cent with a further 2.0 per cent in occupational diseases. The total days unavoidably lost in this way average six or seven annually per man, $\dfrac{30 \times 22\cdot5}{100}$ in addition to the time lost by sickness of six to nine days.

To sum up. *Unavoidable* absence from physical incapacity of all kinds up to twenty-six weeks averages at least six days per year per man and seven and thirteen days for single and for married women in manufacture, and twelve to sixteen days for miners.[1] To this total must be added as unavoidable certain cases, averaging, say, a day a year (but more for married women) where leave is granted, usually for compassionate family reasons.

[1]Ministry of Fuel records give much higher rates of "involuntary absenteeism" but this includes all absence for which a "satisfactory reason" is given.

The *actual* total rates of absence experienced in industry usually exceed these minimum unavoidable rates very considerably. In British coal-mining the rate of absence is published for the industry as a whole. A Royal Commission found that in 1924, twenty-two and three-quarter days per man per year were, in fact, lost by coal-miners. In 1935-38 time lost averaged 6.5 per cent per year or about nineteen and a half days. In 1945 it was 16.3 per cent, or about forty-nine days in the year.

In manufacturing, the average excess of *actual* rates of absence over unavoidable rates are not so high as in mining. The records of firms during the war period of 1914-18 showed actual rates in Britain varying all the way from 5.3 per cent to 14.3 per cent (i.e., sixteen to forty-three work days) for men, and 7.6 per cent to 12.3 per cent (i.e., twenty-three to thirty-seven work days) for women. Contemporary American records did not always distinguish men and women, but an even greater range of variation was shown in men's actual absence rates, from 1.1 per cent (three days) in the offices of a model factory to 17.8 per cent (fifty-three days) in a group of shipyards.[1] Records published in Britain during the Second World War showed the same wide variety. For men, ten factories in Coventry had absence rates varying from nineteen work days per year to forty-two, and in the country generally the secretary of the Industrial Health Research Board reports rates in fifty-two factories varying from fifteen to fifty-one work days per year.[2] For single women the Board reported in two Royal Ordnance Factories a rate of twenty-six and of forty-two days lost per year; and for married women rates of thirty-seven and fifty-nine days per year.

There is thus a wide gap between the actual rates of absence from all causes and the unavoidable days of absence due to sickness and accidents, estimated for manufacturing in normal times as six for men, seven for single and perhaps thirteen for married women. This gap may be partly due to abnormal sickness such as appeared in war-time. Among 3,000 workers in 1943-4, for instance, men were found to lose by physical sickness 2.77 per cent of possible time or about

[1] Florence, *Economics of Fatigue and Unrest*, tables 18, 19 and 20.
[2] *British Journal of Industrial Medicine*, July 1944.

eight work days a year, and women (married and unmarried) 4.06 per cent, or about twelve work days a year. In addition the men were said to have lost 1.09 per cent and the women 2.07 per cent of possible time by neurosis.[1]

Both the abnormal sickness and the avoidable causes not due to physical incapacity, which form the gap between total and normally unavoidable absence, may have their origin in industrial conditions. These conditions may act cumulatively, as when in war-time longer hours are worked by older and less efficient workers under less healthy physical and less attractive social conditions in the factory. Whether action is cumulative or not, abnormal absenteeism is part of the case for prosecuting inquiries into industrial conditions (as in consecutive chapters of Part II) in order to determine their precise influence on labour inefficiency.

§5 STRIKES

Strikes can be measured, like absence, in days lost per year per worker. They are, in fact, organized collective absenteeism and occasion the same unit costs as absence. Unlike absence, however, which may be due either to unwillingness or incapacity of the worker, strikes are by definition due to unwillingness to work under given industrial conditions.

There is a loss of wages for the worker and strike pay granted by the trade union during official strikes does not normally make it up fully. Such strikes are usually announced beforehand and involve the closing of whole departments, so some overhead costs may be saved to the employer. The extent of the aggregate loss is not on an average high compared to absence but may fall heavily on the industries directly involved, or indirectly involved by loss of materials or markets, and the community may suffer great inconvenience if a whole industry or service is stopped.

Official records show that in Britain during the fifteen years 1899 to 1913, strikes in mining, manufacturing, building and transport (employing that half—about 10,000,000—of the working population which is more liable to strike) averaged about two-thirds of a day per year per worker, and in the

[1]Industrial Health Research Board Report 86, p. 12; 90, p. 5.

period 1927-39, before the Second World War, one-third of a day. During the two wars the time lost was somewhat lower than in the previous periods. But in the four years 1919-22 after the First World War, the time lost per worker (among the "strike-liable" 10,000,000) was as high as three and a half, three, eight, and two days; finally, in 1926, with the coal and the General Strike the days lost per worker amounted to sixteen. Clearly the days lost by strikes, though much lower on the average than the days lost by·sickness absence, are more irregular both as between industries and particular periods.

Man-days lost by strikes are also much lower in America than days lost by individual absence and much less stable from year to year. The general level, however, is higher than in England. I have estimated[1] that from 1881 to 1905 on the average 0.38 per cent of total working time (roughly one day per working year) was lost by strikes in the United States, but from 1916 to 1921, 1.25 per cent or about four days per working year. Official statistics from 1927 to 1937 show an annual average of 19,693,000 man-days lost per year. If we estimate the wage earners in the four groups where strikes mainly occur (mining, manufacturing, building and transport) as 17,000,000, the time lost per man was again as in 1881 to 1905 about one day per working year.

Strikes have not directly and in themselves proved very costly to industry as a whole. The main significance of the strike or threat of strike is in the mechanism of collective bargaining (See pp. 190-4) between Trade Unions and employers.

§6 Labour Turnover

The labour turnover rate is usually measured as the number of workers in a year leaving on their own account or discharged from their place of employment and having to be replaced, divided by the total number of workers employed there on the average for the year. Only a few factories tabulate this rate though easily obtainable from records in most factories.[2]

[1]*Economics of Fatigue and Unrest*, p. 191.
[2]The monthly "turnover" rates in *Labour Gazettes* since October, 1948 do not quite tally with this definition. Workers not replaced are included, those replaced within the month excluded, from "labour losses."

In normal times leaving is more frequent than discharge and, like absence and strikes, is obviously an act of the human factor; but it is at first sight less obviously a measure of industrial inefficiency. Indeed, up to a point, leaving indicates the "mobility" between places and industries which is so essential to an efficient national economy. A worker may leave for another industry where his services are nationally in greater demand. On the other hand he may leave for another industry not of that description, or not for another industry at all, but merely for another factory in the same industry, and perhaps the same place.

However low the turnover rate, replacement entails some cost to the employer and eventually to society. This cost lies in the administrative work of replacing the original worker and in training up the new worker to his standard. The trainer must be paid while he teaches others to produce instead of producing himself, and the trainee must be paid at least a living wage though his output may not at first be worth that wage in quantity, quality or economy. Furthermore, new workers are more liable to accident and more liable to leave (thus continuing a vicious circle of turnover) than old-established workers.

The replacement cost varies for different occupations and grades with the value of the equipment and the need for retraining. Labourers and, at the other end of the scale, skilled all-round craftsmen usually have much the same duties in different factories, and do not need the training or use the expensive equipment of semi-skilled workers on specialized machines. It is the growing class of the semi-skilled that is probably the most expensive for the individual factory to replace.

The minimum of labour turnover that cannot be prevented by the employer is due to causes such as death before retirement, retirement, and disablement from illness or injury lasting beyond the period accountable for absence, and taking the worker out of industry altogether. Obviously, the extent of these unavoidable causes depends on the age structure of the workers; the minimum rates of turnover (except for military service will be higher where workers are older.

The only industry where physical causes of unavoidable turnover are published is coal-mining. The age distribution was in 1945 only slightly higher than for industry as a whole, and the details are worth giving:—

CAUSES OF UNAVOIDABLE LABOUR TURNOVER IN COAL MINING
GREAT BRITAIN 1945 (MINISTRY OF FUEL AND POWER)

	Cases	% of Total Employed
Death	3,206	0.4
Retirement	4,646	0.7
Excess of incapacitated over those returning from incapacity ..	39,780	5.6
Total workers on colliery books ..	709,000	100.0

Since new cases of short-term incapacity are balanced by short-term cases returning to industry, the excess of the incapacitated measures new long-term disablement cases, accounting for turnover. In coal mining, however, disability is unusually high. Judging from all-industry samples[1] of disablement cases (with over twenty-six weeks absence from work), turnover due to ill-health is, in manufacture, just over 2 per cent yearly for men and single women, and 4 per cent for married women; incapacity to carry on the original job due to accidents may be estimated for industry (mainly manufacturing) as not more than 1 per cent of those at work. Adding this 2 per cent and 1 per cent to the 0.4 per cent for death and 0.7 per cent for retirement, it appears that for men and single women the minimum unavoidable turnover for physical reasons in manufacturing industry is slightly over 4 per cent per year.

In the case of single women there is the additional risk of retirement on marriage. In occupations and industries where such retirement is customary, the turnover from this cause can be reckoned from the average age of entry of girls (i.e., about fifteen) to the average age of marriage, at present about twenty-five. Even if all women retired on marriage, only one

[1] See Sir A. W. Watson "National Health Insurance: A Statistical Review," Statistical Journal, 1927, Part III.

woman in ten would, on average, leave her employment each year for this reason—yielding a turnover of 10 per cent. The consequences of this risk to the value placed on women's employment is discussed in Chapter X.

The preventable gap between total labour turnover and the minimum unpreventable, consists of workers "quitting" because they are dissatisfied or find more attractive terms elsewhere; and of workers discharged because employers think that, in spite of replacement costs and possible resentment of fellow workers, it will prove less costly to employ a new worker. Discharge (in contrast to workers "laid off" for lack of work and not replaced) is fairly stable from year to year and seldom more than 3 per cent of the working force. In times of industrial depression, avoidable quitting by the worker will also be low (perhaps not more than 5 or 10 per cent) and often less than required for mobility in response to changing demands. But with a high level of employment, as in war-time, quitting when not legally restricted has been recorded as reaching 100 per cent, or even 200 per cent—as many persons, or twice as many persons, leaving a factory and having to be replaced during the year as the number employed there on the average. In fact, a positive correlation can be shown in America between turnover rates and the trade cycle.[1]

The costs of each case of turnover mentioned earlier when multiplied by these percentages may prove a heavy offset to the advantages of full employment. The implication of a policy of "more jobs than men" for a certain proportion of workers continually seeking new jobs has still to be ascertained. Certainly, Russia found that when unemployment had been "liquidated," excessive labour turnover emerged, and controls and penalties had to be imposed on "quitting."[2] The costs to employer and nation may not be those involved in replacement, but rather the difficulty of replacing a worker at all. The consequent idle overhead costs resemble an infinitely prolonged absence cost.

[1]See Florence, *Economics of Fatigue and Unrest*, p. 147 for 1910-19. Watkins and Dodd, *The Management of Labour Relations*, p. 233 for 1929-37.
[2]Baykov, *Soviet Economic System*, p. 361 ff.

High labour turnover and over-mobility from some occupations may occur side by side with immobility from others. Prevention of the relative shortage of labour in some industries because labour stays immobile in others is discussed in Part II, particularly as an aim in wages and in training policy.

§7 UNEMPLOYMENT

Unemployment is the test of inefficiency in the industrial system that has been most widely applied. Records of unemployment are comprehensively summarized officially and, notably in Britain, have been presented as a percentage rate on numbers insured against unemployment, industry by industry, for men and women separately.

Like absence and labour turnover, unemployment is clearly a state of the human factor, but less of an act of choice. Unemployment has been defined as the idleness of a worker willing and able to work. To the unemployed worker the cost is not just the difference between the wages he would have earned if employed and his unemployment benefit. It is, as Lord Beveridge has put it, a "personal catastrophe . . . idleness even on an income corrupts; the feeling of not being wanted demoralizes."[1]

The costs of unemployment fall on the society as well as the worker. It is a waste of perishable national resources and results in a vicious circle. The longer a worker is unemployed the less fit and efficient he will be for further work and the more likely to remain unemployed. But the waste of human resources is not paid for by the employer. An unemployed worker's last employer does not necessarily have to replace him, and none of the retraining costs and interim loss of output due to labour turnover are involved.

What is the preventable gap between unavoidable and total unemployment? However accurately the internal economy of a country is planned, unemployment is unavoidable (given a certain immobility of labour) owing to seasonal fluctuations, uncertainties of the export trade and change of employment incidental to progress. Allowing 1 per cent for each of these three factors, it has been thought possible to reduce the

[1] *Full Employment in a Free Society* (1944) p. 19.

unemployment rate to an average of 3 per cent of insured workers.[1] But this calculation neglects the fact that among the legally insured population there is a certain percentage unfit for the work which they are seeking, and continually in and out of jobs. If there were a thorough general medical examination, these cases could be advised to seek more suitable jobs, or could be excluded altogether from the labour market and treated medically until they were fit. But under existing circumstances they must be added to the numerator of the unemployment percentage, as they are to the denominator, thus adding an uncertain amount to the average of 3 per cent for the unemployment of the genuinely fit under full employment.

In the recent past, unemployment rates have been greatly in excess of this unpreventable minimum. For industry generally over the whole of Britain a peak of unemployment was reached in August 1932 of 23·1 per cent, but regionally much higher rates have been recorded such as (again in August 1932) 39.1 per cent for Wales and 30.9 per cent in the North Eastern region. Still higher percentages have been recorded for particular industries over the whole country, notably, among the larger industries in August 1932: jute 41.1 per cent; coal mining 41.6 per cent; tin-plate 45.6 per cent; marine engineering 50.2 per cent; iron and steel 49.3 per cent; shipbuilding 59.8 per cent.

Unemployment has been and might again become a heavy, yet preventable, loss; and it is a loss falling mainly on the worker and the community. The industrial means towards its prevention are discussed in Part III in some detail. They include the local diversification of industry and State investment policy, as well as the encouragement of greater mobility of labour.

[1]Beveridge, op. cit., p. 128.

PART II

LABOUR IN EMPLOYMENT

CHAPTER IV

HOURS OF EMPLOYMENT

§1 FATIGUE, DURATION AND INTENSITY OF WORK

THE scientific study of the terms of employment making for labour efficiency has gone further in exploring the effect of hours of work than perhaps any other condition. As early as 1900 Ernst Abbé tested the effect of reducing hours per day from nine to eight at the Zeiss Works in Jena, of which he was manager. In 1912 Miss Josephine Goldmark was able to compile her "Fatigue and Efficiency" summarizing many experiments in England, France, Belgium and America, and in 1913 the British Association for the Advancement of Science appointed a committee for investigating "the question of fatigue from the economic standpoint." If fatigue is defined as relative incapacity due to excessive activity continuously undergone, it is clearly related particularly to duration and intensity of activity, and while hours of work were long, fatigue remained a dominant interest to investigators.

At the outbreak of the First World War, hours of work even of women were often raised in Britain to seventy-two hours a week, and this period produced the classical series of inquiries into long hours, summed up in the next two sections. The inquiries were sponsored by the Health of Munition Workers Committee, later converted into the Industrial Fatigue Research Board, which in turn changed its title to Industrial Health Research Board.

Since 1919 in Britain, when the forty-eight-hour week was generally introduced, and since 1933 in America when still shorter hours became the rule, interest has passed from

49

aggregate hours to problems of speeding-up and intensity of work and the incidence and distribution of hours—i.e., the five-day week, holidays with pay, rest pauses, shiftwork. Distribution of hours will be discussed in the last section of this chapter; but a word must here be said about intensity of work.

The excessive activity to which fatigue is attributed may be excessive either in duration or in intensity, and in recent years the shortening of the duration of work may well have been offset by increasing intensity of work. Intensity has been increased (a) mechanically by direct speeding up of machines, conveyor belts, etc., or by additional requirements, e.g., loading up the worker with more machines to mind; (b) by speeding up organization, e.g., through cutting out time wasted bringing up materials or repairing equipment; (c) more indirectly, by strengthening incentives to the worker, e.g., in the form of piece-wages; (d) by closer supervision of the worker and recording of his output. The effect of incentives and supervision is reviewed in Chapters VI and VIII; the need of compensating for speed-up in organization is discussed later under rest pauses, but the effect on output, spoiled work and accidents of mechanical and organizational speed-up has only been fragmentarily studied, though some of the fragments show interesting results.

Machines which require continuous feeding or stocking with raw material set, when speeded up, a proportionately higher target for the operator, and targets may be raised with resultant increase in output up to a point; but, when speeded up beyond that point, output may fall. The Industrial Health Research Board found, for instance (Report 82) that in feeding slabs of toffee into slots on a dial mechanically speeded, output was not proportional to increases in machine speed—a fact largely due to the inability of the operator to keep the machine supplied with the toffee. "At the lower speeds the operator usually had time to break and feed the toffee into the machine, but at the higher speeds it became increasingly necessary to stop the machine for this purpose. Stoppages of this type were particularly frequent at the highest speed when it was evident that the workers showed signs of fatigue and strain." Fatigue was indicated by a sharp fall in the output toward the end of the working day. The Board's report recommended not only limits to mechanical speeding up that will take account of the average capacity of the group, but adjustment of each machine to the ascertained capacity of the single operator. Studies have also been made of the effect of "loading up" with much the same indication of an optimum scheduled load beyond which actual output falls.

§2 EFFECT OF CHANGED HOURS

The direct method of testing the efficiency of various hours of work is obviously to compare the output, lost time or accidents before and after a change in hours, making certain that no other conditions are changed. Unfortunately employers, when they change their hours, usually change other conditions as well, especially wages or methods of paying them, and in any case do not keep records before as well as after the change. So recorded observations on change in hours where the factors are scientifically isolated and controlled are few in number. The most famous are Abbé's experiment in the eight-hour day and H. M. Vernon's analysis of records at British munition factories in 1915-18.

In 1900 Abbé altered the scheduled hours at the Zeiss Optical Works at Jena, from nine to eight per day, and carefully observed the power consumed in driving the machinery for four weeks before and after the change. This power was found to have increased some 12 per cent per hour. As a further check Abbé compared the piece-rate earnings of the employees for a year before and after the change, and found them to have increased 16.2 per cent per hour. Factors other than the hours of work had been kept constant, and Abbé felt justified in attributing the former low productivity specifically to the longer hours. Eight hours' work at a rate of 116.2 per cent of the hourly output on the nine-hour schedule implies mathematically a daily output of 8×116.2 or 929.6 compared with a daily output of 900 on the nine-hour schedule—a rise of 3.3 per cent.

Vernon's series of observations have been quoted over and over again since they were published in various memoranda of the Health of Munition Workers Committee, and summarized in its final report (1919, Cd. 9065). He found four operations, two performed by women, one by men, and one by boys, on standard parts of the shell-fuse carried on (and the output recorded) over a long period during which successive reductions in hours had been made. At the outset of the First World War the British War Office assumed that output would be directly in proportion to hours worked and asked for a twelve-hour day at least six days a week. Vernon's analysis shows up the error of this assumption. On each of the operations studied reductions in hours produced a considerably increased hourly output, so much so that in spite of large reductions in total hours the total weekly output rose or remained roughly constant. Since results do not differ greatly, observations on two of the operations may be presented in Table 6 as fairly representative; eighty to ninety-five women turning aluminium fuse bodies on capstan lathes, which involved the application in succession of seven cutting and boring tools; fifty-six men sizing fuse bodies, which involved screwing the bodies by hand into a steel tap. The rise in weekly output with nominal hours shorter by 19.2 and 10.2 than the original period, is seen (in the third periods) to be 13 and 22 per cent over the original period.

Hours as long as in the original period recorded by Vernon are no longer worked to-day except when overtime is added to the normal day. Unfortunately little research has recently been done on the effect of overtime. In 1919 I observed in America the increase in total output associated with the addition of two and two-third hours overtime to a normal ten-hour day. Compared to a normal day after a normal day there was a fall of 6.5 per cent in the hourly rate of output on days with overtime and a fall of 3.9 per cent on the normal days after overtime days—possibly due to "hang-over" fatigue. During overtime piece-wages were paid at one and a half times the normal rate and the low average hourly output for the whole day was apparently due to workers reserving their strength in the normal period for cashing in during the better paid overtime. Thus in the two days, including a period of overtime, a considerably reduced hourly output was paid for by an average hourly wage considerably increased.[1]

[1]Florence, *Economics of Fatigue and Unrest*, pp. 230-2.

TABLE 6: COMPARATIVE OUTPUT FROM LONGER AND SHORTER HOURS OF WORK, 1915-17

	Average Weekly Hours Nominal[1]	Actual	Relative Hourly	Output Weekly
80-95 Women turning Fuse Bodies on Capstan Lathes[2]:				
First Period—				
Aug. 15-Jan 16	74.5	66.0	100	100
Second Period—				
Jan. 16-July 30	63.5	54.4	121	100
Third Period—				
July 30-May 5	55.3	47.5	156	113
56 Men Sizing Fuse Bodies:[3]				
First Period—				
Nov. 14-Dec. 19	66.7	58.2	100	100
Second Period—				
Feb. 27-Apr. 16	62.8	50.5	122	106
Third Period—				
Nov. 11-Dec. 23	56.5	51.2	139	122

Long hours appear to affect accidents and lost time, no less than output, though here it is more difficult to isolate long hours from other factors. Vernon found that women working on a seventy-five-hour week had 228 per cent the accidents per hour, than when working on alternate 64½ and 58½-hour weeks.[4] Table 6 shows that as the nominal hours spent in the factory are reduced, the time lost inside the factory was often reduced out of proportion. The men sizing, for instance, lost only 5.3 hours a week when on a 56.5 hour schedule, as against

[1]Nominal means hours spent in the factory; actual means nominal minus time lost in the factory for various reasons.
[2]H. M. Vernon, *Industrial Fatigue and Efficiency*, p. 39.
[3]Industrial Health Research Board, Emergency Report No. 1.
[4]H. M. Vernon, *Accidents and Their Prevention*, pp. 67-9.

12.3 when on a 62.8-hour schedule. Actual absence from work
was also shown during both world wars to rise and fall (often
with some lag) with lengthened and shortened hours. In 1915
with the continuance of twelve-hour shifts, imposed in September 1914, women's lost time in a large shipyard and munition
plant rose 30 per cent above 1914 for the same autumn months.[1]
In 1940-41, to quote the conclusions of the Industrial Health
Research Board emergency report issued in 1942:

The time lost by factory workers through sickness, injury and
absence without permission, when undisturbed by extraneous
factors, varied with the weekly hours of work. It was usually low
when hours of work were less than sixty per week but increased as
the hours increased up to seventy-five.

§3 THE WORK CURVE

When no alteration is made in the schedule of hours, it is
still possible to study the effect of hours of work by the device
of the work curve. The curve is obtained by plotting the output
or the spoiled work or the accidents occurring over stated
intervals throughout a working period. The most usual and
useful curve is obtained by plotting these tests of efficiency at
hourly intervals throughout the working day. Since few changes
are made in factory organization in the course of the day, these
curves automatically isolate the factor of previous activity;
changes in the hourly rate of output or accidents as the working
day proceeds will reflect lengthening of previous hours of
work and, except for the time of day and the approach and
effect of meal times, little else. Table 7 gives a number of such
curves for an American metal factory which normally worked a
ten-hour day from seven to twelve and one to six. The
left-hand table (7A) distinguishes accident and output
curves for different types of work and will be discussed in the
next chapter; it is the right-hand table (7B), giving the general
effect of long hours, which must be considered here.

Output was obtained from some twenty different operations
selected as representative samples of various types of work on
each of which perhaps six to a dozen workers were observed for
two or three weeks. The percentage of work spoiled, difficult

[1]Florence, op. cit., pp. 206-8.

to obtain hour by hour, refers only to one operation, grinding springs, and the accident records refer to all accidents (however slight the injury) occurring to the workers in the factory over a period of three years. It is not the absolute accident figures that are plotted, but the ratio of accidents to output, as obtained by the output curve. The reason for this adjustment is that as output rises accidents may be expected to rise at least proportionately, and it is the variation in the risk per unit of output rather than the crude number of accidents that is significant of the effect of hours.

Four conclusions follow from an inspection of these curves:

(1) As activity proceeds throughout the day there is finally a fall in quantity of output, a rise in spoiled work and a very considerable rise in accidents, all of which are indicative of fatigue. The last hour of the day has the lowest output and highest accident ratio and the general level of the afternoon spell is lower for output and higher for accidents than that of the morning spell.

(2) These fatigue effects are also noticeable within each continuous spell of work. Output curves turn down and spoiled work curves up in the course of the morning as well as the afternoon spell.

(3) Other processes are at work as well as the "fatigue" occurring toward the end of a spell's or day's activity. At the start of the day output is low and spoiled work high, indicative of a settling down, warming up or practice effect postulated by psychologists—though this does not influence accidents. Accidents, however, show a curious fall in the last hour of the morning spell—an effect noticed in other records which I have attributed to anticipation of a meal break that may give added alertness to the workers.[1]

(4) The meal break raises the rate of output and lowers the accident rate and spoilage. On the whole, lowered efficiency appears not only associated with long hours

[1]An interpretation in which I am, not unanimously supported. The whole interpretation of accident curves is still a matter of controversy, see especially Vernon, *Accidents and Their Prevention*, pp. 64-70 and my article and review, *Economic Journal*, June 1923 and June 1937.

TABLE 7(A): HOUR BY HOUR CURVES OF ACCIDENTS AND OUTPUT ON DIFFERENT TYPES OF WORK

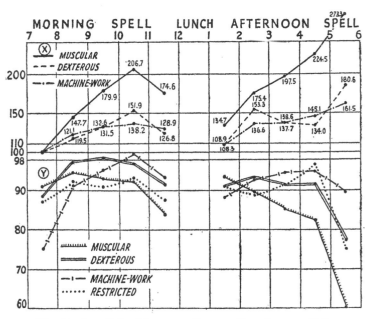

X=Ratio of Accidents to Output (first hour=100)
Y=Relative Hourly Output (limit of efficiency=100)

TABLE 7(B): HOUR BY HOUR GENERAL CURVES
OF OUTPUT, RATIO OF ACCIDENTS, AND SPOILED
WORK COMPARED (Average = 100)

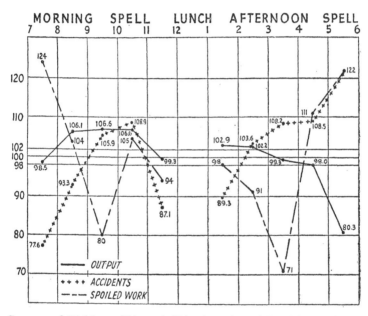

Source of Table 7 (A) and (B), American Ten Hour Plant,
See P. S. Florence, Economics of Fatigue and Unrest, p. 351

previously worked over the complete day but also with the hours worked continuously without a break. This is confirmed by the fact that no typical characteristic weekly day-by-day curves of output or accidents have been obtained. The long break between days provided by an evening's relaxation and a night's sleep appears sufficient to reconstitute the output and accident rate of each working day. The daily hour-by-hour curves in the right section of Table 7, on the other hand, are typical, and significant of the effects of continuous activity—though as the next chapter will reveal and the left section of the table shows, there are characteristic variations for different types of work.

A similar series of work curves were obtained simultaneously for an American factory (Ford's original plant at Detroit) working the eight-hour day.[1] Here the curves on the same types of work were more stable, but there were still signs of fatigue at the end of the working day in lower output and more frequent accidents.

Summing up in 1924 with the results of the experience of the First World War fully published and discussed,[2] I claimed the forty-eight-hour week as "probably the optimum length of hours for ordinary business efficiency." Though "in the case of a large proportion of industrial operations, where mechanical forces set the speed of work, longer hours might possibly be more productive," there are "economic advantages in shorter hours which would outweigh the disadvantages of a slightly smaller output." Among these advantages are:—

(1) Stability of output throughout the day.
(2) Less lost time, accidents and spoiled work in proportion to output.
(3) A saving of overhead costs, such as heating, lighting, and power for driving shafting, that are proportionate to scheduled hours, and not to output.

Besides these economic considerations affecting the employer's profit and loss account, certain national long-run criteria

[1] *U.S. Public Health Bulletin* 106.
[2] "The Forty-eight Hour Week and Industrial Efficiency," *International Labour Review*, November 1924.

must also be borne in mind. Though he may produce slightly less per day, it is of national advantage to prolong the working years of the individual as compared to his childhood and to his period of senility and retirement from work, when he is a national liability rather than an asset. This long-run national criterion of maximum output per working life, which may call for shorter hours per day, does not apply, however, in periods of short-run emergency when, as during a war, immediate efficiency is the need, even if it is effected at the expense of some shortening of working lives in the future.

Since 1924 the case for shorter hours has been strengthened by the increasing speeding and loading up referred to in §1 as well as the longer journeys from home to work (described in Chapter IX) which many workers have to undertake. If a forty-eight-hour week was on the whole the long-run optimum for efficiency in 1924, a forty-four-hour week may now be so. In 1948 weekly hours of men mainly manufacturing averaged forty-six and a half, and of women forty-one and a half. How were these distributed, and what observations made on the effect of the introduction of rest pauses, the five-day week and multiple shifts?

§4 The Distribution of Hours of Work; Week-ends, Pauses and Shifts

Hours of work policies under discussion at the present time are concerned largely with the arrangement or distribution of a given total of hours, rather than with the grand overall total. The five-day week and two-day week-end may or may not involve a reduction of weekly hours, and the policy of rest pauses is designed to give a short break in continuous spells of work rather than to reduce hours. Even the policy of working multiple shifts is essentially one of rearrangement, though it often carries with it a shortening of total hours. These three devices which figure so largely in modern controversy must therefore seek a scientific basis on their own merits; they are not mere applications of one general rule for or against shorter hours.

Assuimng the same total length of the working week, the special argument for the five-day week is that the Saturday half-day is often uneconomical because of lower output per

hour and more absenteeism; and because (if workers live a
long distance from their work) it is wasteful for them to come
all the way from home and back merely for a morning's work.
The five-day working week is particularly economical of effort
in large towns, therefore, where many workers come from long
distances. It is noticeable, however, that when a vote is taken
girls are not so keen on the five-day week as men and boys.
This may be due to their mothers making them do housework
on the Saturday morning, instead of allowing complete relaxation. Assuming, however, a full two-day relaxation the long
week-end may give an anticipatory stimulus to efficiency
similar to that before the annual holiday (which goes to justify
another recent innovation, holidays with pay). The main argument against the five-day week without reduction of total
weekly hours is the length of hours in each of the spells of the
five working days. A forty-eight-hour week split equally into
five workdays involves nine and three-fifths hours per day,
with one of the two spells of the day probably five hours long.

This brings up the main argument for the rest pause or
break, namely the fatigue and boredom engendered by a long
spell of unbroken work. Where spells are more than four hours
long, a considerable falling off in output has been shown to
occur in their final hour and, in the next chapter, other work
curves will be shown with a considerable dip in output in their
middle. The falling-off, usually attributed to fatigue, occurs
particularly where piece rates are paid and the work is heavy;
the mid-spell dip, attributed to boredom, occurs particularly
where time rates are paid and the worker is not stimulated to
work hard. Both fatigue and boredom appear to be reducible
by rest pauses.

Before the advent of mass-production and factory rationali-
zation it was normal for workers to get rests involuntarily
through slack organization, or to take surreptitious rests voluntarily. These rests have been observed to last longer, the more
strenuous the work. Clearly it would be unwise by stern
discipline to stop the voluntary pauses, or by efficiency methods
to eliminate the involuntary pauses, without providing officially
some compensatory rest periods. Yet the speeding up described
in §1 often involves such unwisdom. It would be equally unwise

to "load" up by increasing the heaviness or responsibilities of the work demanded of a worker without giving additional rests. Frederick Taylor when he increased the load of pig-iron handled by the ox-like Schmitt gave him rest-periods amounting to half his time.[1]

In light work pauses do not have to be so long, but they are still of value to efficiency in relieving the feeling of monotony and keeping up the output curve when it would otherwise fall. In fact, the point at which the output begins to drop gives a useful indication of the right time to introduce the pause.

The introduction of rest pauses, usually of ten minutes in the middle of the spell, is quite a frequent policy, at least in Britain. Among 1,050 factories chosen at random in seven different areas in 1938, 53 per cent had official rest pauses, 15 per cent admitted there were unofficial pauses.[2] Actual results of rest pauses upon output have been reported in a number of official publications starting with U.S. Public Health Bulletin 106, and continuing through reports 41, 42 and 47 of the Industrial Health Research Board. The American investigators obtained increased output when rest pauses were inserted in five-hour spells, but not in four-hour spells. Reviewing investigations in the lighter industries over a period of eighteen years, the Industrial Health Research Board concluded that "a pause of five to ten minutes given about the middle of the work spell was found to increase output by 5 to 10 per cent."[3] The actual percentages of changes in output, comparing the period before the introduction of the pause with a period some months later (when the workers have presumably become adapted to the pause) show considerable variation between one operation and another. Out of fourteen operations observed by Vernon and others, one showed a fall in output; otherwise the changes were all increases, varying from 0.2 per cent to 13 per cent.

These increases in output are attributed by the Board "not only to the decrease in the number of voluntary rests observed, but also to the diminution in boredom and fatigue, inducing a

[1]*Principles of Scientific Management*, pp. 40-64.
[2]J. Ramsay, R. E. Rawson and others, *Rest Pauses and Refreshments in Industry*. National Institute of Industrial Psychology.
[3]18th Annual Report.

higher rate of working. There is also an incentive effort when a pause is expected; work improves for some time before the moment the rest comes, but the physiological effects of rest pauses are chiefly due to the enforced changes of posture and activity." The incentive or anticipatory effect of a pause is indicated by typical remarks of the workers themselves. "It used to help a lot when you knew you were having a break— you put on a spurt before the break and afterwards you worked well to the end." "We used to look forward to the rest and afterwards time seemed to fly." "Rests were the two bright spots of the day."

More important than the five-day week or rest pauses for the future of the whole national economy is the working of multiple shifts. When machines and equipment are becoming more and more important in production and liable by the pace of invention to become more quickly out of date, it is essential that the fixed overhead expense of obsolescence and of depreciation through exposure should be reduced to the minimum cost *per unit* by a maximum total output from each machine. This involves working machines long hours, possibly sixteen or even twenty-four hours per day. Since the human factor is limited by fatigue and cannot work efficiently much more than eight hours, the obvious solution is to use several shifts of workers on the same machine, possibly two or three eight-hour shifts or even four six-hour shifts. Six-hour shifts were advocated by Lord Leverhulme in his "Six-Hour Day" essays, and four six-hour shifts are actually worked in some factories, notably Kellogg's at Battle Creek.

Working machines round the clock involves night-work, the introduction of which is likely to prove unpopular in industries not accustomed to it. From the standpoint of health and efficiency the main factor is disturbed sleep. A study of women on night-work during the recent war revealed that only 14.5 per cent of them rested for more than eight hours in the twenty-four. In the First World War a number-of-men-asleep curve was worked out in an American factory department during the latter part of a twelve-hour night shift.[1] Where it is possible, sleep at work may offset lack of sleep at home.

[1] *U.S. Public Health Bulletin* 106, p. 154.

If night-work is objected to, it would still help national efficiency if only two shifts of eight or perhaps seven hours were introduced even though the wages per shift remained the same. It may be concluded from the preceding sections and from specific observation of shifts,[1] that output per hour will be higher with the shorter hours, but not quite sufficient to make the total output of seven equal to an eight hours' output. Let us make the likely assumption that total output is 5 per cent less. The two seven-hour shifts will then produce 95 per cent $\times$ 2=190 per cent of the original eight-hour single shift. Assuming, as Lord Leverhulme did, that the costs of fixed overhead is the same as the cost of wages on a single shift, then the cost per unit of output on the one-shift and on the two-shift systems can be compared as follows:

	One Shift of Eight Hours.	Two Shifts of Seven Hours.
Aggregate Cost of Fixed Overheads	£1,000	£1,000
Aggregate Cost of Wages ..	£1,000	£2,000
Total Cost	£2,000	£3,000
Units of Output Produced ..	1,000	1,900
Cost per Unit of Output ..	£2	£1.58

Two shifts have thus reduced hours of the workers, maintained wages and cut down cost by more than a fifth.

Though two seven-hour day shifts could be conveniently arranged within the span of a worker's normal waking hours (say, from 7.30 to 3.15 with a three-quarter-hour lunch break from 11.30 to 12.15, and from 3.15 to 11 with a three-quarter-hour supper break between 7 and 7.45) the chief objection to shifts comes from the workers. While the employer may find some difficulty in co-ordinating the two foremen in charge of the two shifts in the same department, and in fixing responsibility for upkeep or for use of tools on each of the shift-workers on the same machine; the difficulties in the worker's attitude are more fundamental. One objection is against a time-pattern

[1]Industrial Health Research Board Report, 24; Vernon, *The Shorter Working Day.*

of life different to the present norm. The afternoon shift in particular will prevent the normal evening recreation. Another objection is to segregation so that friends may find themselves on different shifts. A third objection is that if members of her household work on different shifts the housewife will have to be preparing meals all hours of the day, and also sleep may be hard to get in the home.

The first objection can be overcome by rotating the shifts so that workers can sometimes be on the morning shift with its conformity to the usual pattern of life. Rotation, however, introduces new objections, namely, physiological disturbances when meal times change (which appears to result in loss of efficiency) and disturbance to social arrangements such as courses of lectures at fixed times throughout a session.

Nevertheless rotating shift systems usually covering night as well as day have worked successfully in continuous process industries such as iron and steel, glass-making, gas or electricity supply, and there is no reason why workers' objections cannot be met in other industries. The fact that economies in machine costs allow shorter total hours of work should influence many workers. Some workers may prefer the afternoon shift since it gives more hours of leisure in daylight; but if an insufficient number prefer it, the attraction of a five-day week in afternoon shifts as against a six-day week in morning shifts may persuade the necessary remainder.[1] In any case though the number to work on each shift must be fixed by the management, the actual persons to fill the quota may be left to the voluntary choice of the workers.

Shift work may also contribute to the easing of man-power shortage in so far as shifts of part-time workers can take the place of a single full-time worker. The largest source of potential industrial man-power not used is the married woman, and married women without young children may well be induced to enter industry if their hours are limited to, say, four, thus permitting house and factory work to be combined—double duty without tears.

[1] The Committee on Double Day-Shift Working (1947) report (*see* Cmd. 7147) against all Saturday work; but this throws away the chance of offering the attractive of shorter weekly hours to the afternoon shift.

CHAPTER V

PHYSICAL CONDITIONS AND TYPES OF WORK

§1 Effect of Hours on Efficiency for Different Types of Work

The call which work makes upon the human factor and the consequent efficiency of labour varies greatly according to the type of work. The call may be upon the muscles, the nerves, the senses or the brain according as the work is heavy, irregular, inspecting rather than doing, or to be adapted to circumstance rather than uniform. Some of these types of work can be measurably distinguished by weighing the materials handled, timing the recurrence and regularity of recurrence of operations and so on. Different physical environments—cold, heat, dampness, noise—also influence the efficiency of labour and can be measured for purposes of correlating conditions and results on output, accidents, lost time and turnover.

This section will point to the effect of different types of work in influencing the bearing of hours of work upon output and accident. The hourly work curves described in the previous chapter were mostly obtained in a large mechanized American metal factory, largely making brassware and munitions. In this factory I was able to analyse the entire series of operations performed, as shown in Table 8, according to their uniformity, or to that need for adaptation to circumstances entailed by the work of the craftsman or the administrator. If uniform, processes can be subdivided into those where man works with a machine (accounting for 35.8 per cent of all operations in Table 8), or without. If man works without a machine further subdivision is by the parts of the body called upon, for instance, brain, hand, senses, or body generally. If machines are used human interest fastens on the precise part the worker plays. He may (to mention the more significant cases) drive the machine with his own power, or operate the various tools at his own speed, or merely tend the machine, supervising its

65

C

automatic operation and (like a nurse to a child) supplying it at certain intervals with materials to consume.

TABLE 8: TYPES OF OCCUPATION IN A METAL FACTORY

Designation	Example	Per cent of Employees so occupied		
Uniform Processes				
1. Brain work	Clerks			3.9
2. Hand work	Bench-assembly			10.2
3. Sense work	Inspecting, gauging			13.7
4. Body work	Labour			16.3
5. Machine work—				
(*a*) Man-driven	Foot-presses		1.4	
(*b*) Man-steered	Cranes		1.3	
(*c*) Man-operated	Lathes		13.8	
(*d*) Man-fed	Grinding-wheels		0.8	
(*e*) Man-stocked	Dial-feed presses		2.6	
(*f*) Man-tended				
i. Chemical Treatment	Furnaces	9.0		
ii. Mechanical Treatment	Automatics	6.9		
			— 15.9	
				—— 35.8
Adaptable Processes				
6. Crafts—				
(*a*) Stationary	Toolmakers		5.6	
(*b*) Circulating	Toolsetters		4.1	
(*c*) Structural	Building, maintenance		5.9	
			—— 15.6	
7. Custodial	Police, watchmen			2.5
8. Administrative	Executives, foremen			2.0
All processes				100.0

It was possible to obtain sufficient data from the particular factory whose operations are analysed in Table 8 to draw output and accident curves for three sorts of work; dexterous, muscular and machine work. Dexterous work is synonymous with hand work in Table 8 (line 2); muscular work includes body work (4) and man-driven machines (5a), as well as helpers lifting heavy materials connected with machine work; machine work covers the remaining machine workers. Other types of work shown in Table 8 not being uniform processes, or (if uniform) not producing physical output, were not amenable to the measurement of output, and on the whole had relatively few accidents.

The hourly curves of output, and of accidents related to this output, are divided, then, in the left half of Table 7 into three types of work. Comparing these curves, the theory that fatigue is at work is reinforced by the fact that the continuous fall in output and the rise in accidents as the working day proceeds is much greater on the heavy muscular work than on the lighter dexterous and machine work. The effect of initial lack of practice appears more readily overcome on the muscular work than on machine work.

These curves for three types of work were collected during the First World War and since then other types have had their work curves studied. Inspection processes show considerable falling off in speed and accuracy during the spell of work, and there is reason to believe that uninterrupted hours tell especially on the quality of work requiring close attention. More clearly identified is the curve on monotonous work which shows for each spell a saddle- or camel's-back curve with two humps. The events represented by this curve are described by the Industrial Health Research Board's 18th Annual Report:—

There is "a sluggish start before the worker is warmed up, a sharp rise as he gets into his stride, a flagging in the middle of the spell, a fresh spurt—with an eye on the clock—as the spell nears its end, with a final falling off in the last hour. . . . The central drop is more marked in charts of light repetitive work where it is attributed to boredom."

This drop in output coincides in time with subjective feelings of monotony to which workers have given expression.

The feelings are probably due to the lack of any rest or any prospect of change that can be anticipated in the middle of the spell. The reduced rate of working noticeable about the middle of the spell and attributed to boredom usually last from one to two hours and during that time the average reduction in the rate of working varies from 5 to 10 per cent.

The saddle-back curves were chiefly obtained by the Board where time wages were paid, whereas most of the curves obtained during the First World War were on piece wages when, as will be shown in Chapter VIII, incentives are stronger and more sustained. Differences in the shape of the work curve must therefore not be attributed solely to differences in type of work. In fact, one of the work curves given in the left half of Table 7 shows how deliberate restriction of output will outweigh other factors—a matter discussed in Chapters VI-VIII. It is probable that when the incentive to work is weak, fatigue effects such as a continuous fall in output toward the end of work will not be observed.

§2 THE HEALTHINESS OF OCCUPATIONS

Industrial work varies widely in the call made upon the human factor, and so do the physical conditions connected with work. Some occupations like agriculture, building and transport must be carried on out of doors; others, like mining, below ground; others, like most manufacturing and all shop and office work, indoors. Work out of doors involves sudden change of temperature and the risk of a wetting; work underground, heat and often stagnant air and lighting problems; while work indoors depends for its physical conditions more on man-made plans which can be adjusted to human needs.

Differences in physical environment (including materials worked with), together with the differences in type of work, result in wide variation in the degree of health among the workers and in the types of ill-health—a variation brought out by standardized mortality ratios of men occupied, between the ages of twenty and sixty-five[1]. To take only the larger occupational groups in England in 1930-32, clergymen of the Anglican church, bank and insurance officials, civil servants

[1]The Registrar-General's Decennial Supplement, 1937, Part IIa.

and farmers had between 66 and 73 per cent of the average mortality rate of all occupied men; but potters had 135 per cent, metal grinders 137 per cent, metal glaziers, polishers, buffers and moppers 144 per cent, cotton strippers and grinders 145 per cent, barmen 149 per cent, and hotel-keepers 155 per cent. Figures published by the Registrar-General every ten years, from which these extreme cases are quoted, compare and "rank" nearly two hundred occupations in order of death rates, and it is possible to trace certain mortal and certain healthy conditions common to high- and to low-rank occupations. The most deadly is silica dust present in the work of potters and of metal polishers and grinders; and *apparently*, conditions in bars and inns are none too healthy—though the possibility must not be over-looked of many already ill selecting innkeeping as a comfortable billet. On the other hand, open-air work such as the farmer's, and an income not too low, such as the clergyman's, the civil servant's or the bank and insurance official's, are shown to make for a longer life.

High death rates are an indication of industrial inefficiency since they suggest conditions causing early disablement, retire-ment from work, a higher labour turnover, and some previous periods of sickness resulting in absence. Direct measures of disablement and sickness absence among different occupations are not comprehensively collected, but some studies have been made in particular occupations where health hazards were suspected. Table 9 gives results of inquiries based on the claims to sick benefit under the British National Health Insurance scheme. It will be seen that rates of disablement or sickness absence for any occupation may be unusually high for one particular age group, such as for young compositors compared to the general sample of all industries (given in the two top lines) or for older cotton workers in the card room compared to other departments, such as the ring room. To find effective measures of prevention the exact type of disease accounting for the abnormal disablement or sickness absence can and should be followed up from the published records. Thus the young compositors and the older card room workers were found to have a high incidence of tuberculosis and respiratory diseases

TABLE 9: SHORT-TERM SICKNESS AND LONG-TERM DISABLEMENT RATES IN VARIOUS TYPES OF WORK

ANNUAL CALENDAR DAYS PER PERSON, OF SICKNESS AND OF DISABLEMENT ABSENCE.[1]

Occupation	Men Aged			Widows and Single Women Aged 50-69
	16-19	50-54	55-59	
General Sample (1921-3)				
Sickness (see Table 16)	4.41	7.70	9.73	—
Disablement	0.63	5.53	9.87	—
Printing: Compositors (1921-3)				
Sickness	4.77	4.56	5.84	—
Disablement	1.53	3.07	8.24	—
		Aged 50-59	Aged 60-69	
Cotton Spinning (1923-7) Ring room and Warehouse				
Sickness	4.89	5.81	16.48	12.46
Card room				
Sickness	4.41	10.61	20.51	17.25

respectively indicating a need for medical examination when selecting young compositors and for attention to air and dust conditions in the composing and the card rooms. The card room differs from the ring room and warehouse in the presence of dust from the cotton waste.

Some types of disease like miner's nystagmus, or miner's beat hand or beat knee, or dermatitis occurring in manufacturing, are particularly connected with certain occupations.

[1]Absence under and over twenty-six weeks respectively. Source—Industrial Health Research Board Reports 54, 59.

Workers suffering from such "occupational diseases" are compensated like those injured by industrial accident and the cases are recorded as in Table 3. Among miners, cases of occupational disease average yearly about 2 per cent of the total of workers. The proportion is less than one per 1,000 in every other industrial group, but most of these cases are serious and last longer than accidents.

§3 ANALYSIS OF PHYSICAL CONDITIONS

Attention has already been drawn to the presence of certain dusts from metals or cotton waste as dangerous to life, but, further hazards to health, to sickness absence and to efficiency generally, can be found in air, noise and lighting conditions. Factories were (and still are) built to accommodate machinery and to protect industrial materials and processes, not primarily for the health of the workers. Hence the worker will find conditions making for technical efficiency like a humid atmosphere for cotton-spinning, and conditions resulting from technical processes like fumes, heat, noise, glare and dust; but he will not necessarily find conditions (such as sufficient cover from the weather and protection from machinery) for his own health and safety—or even efficiency. The exhortation of Robert Owen to take at least as much care of the human as the mechanical factor quoted in Chapter II, has yet to be appreciated by the majority of employers.

Where factories are organized into a number of departments with very different physical conditions, comparisons can be instituted between their similarly recorded turnover and absence rates. Table 10 gives an example from the Ford automobile plant in Detroit investigated in 1917-18 for the effects of air, noise and other conditions.[1] Here workers were allowed to request transfer from one department to another, so that the rate per hundred workers of transfers requested and granted could be added to the measures of labour efficiency. The physical conditions of each department were tested as objectively as possible by independent investigators; in all the five noisy departments, for example, there was such a racket that the investigators could not hear themselves speak. The figures

[1] *U.S. Public Health Bulletin* 106, p. 159-163.

TABLE 10: COMPARISON OF EFFICIENCY OF DEPARTMENTS WITH EXTREME PHYSICAL CONDITIONS AS AGAINST GENERAL AVERAGE

AMERICAN AUTOMOBILE PLANT

Average of all 65 departments:	Percentage of working-force per month			Percentage of time lost
	Transfers Requested 7.76	Transfers granted .38	Turn-over 1·12	6·13
13 Depts. with Bad Air Conditions:	11.73	·43	1·39	6·45
5 Depts. with Great Noise:	10·37	·40	1·28	6·82
9 Depts. with work involving Eye-strain:	9·13	·50	1·14	6·29

show that the averages of requests for transfer, of transfers granted, of turnover and of lost time in departments where workers had to endure noise, bad air conditions, and eye-strain owing to fine work are each higher than the average for all departments.

The air of a workplace may lead to inefficient labour because it is too hot or too cold, too humid or too dry, too draughty or too stagnant. Now degrees of heat, humidity and stagnancy can all be accurately measured by appropriate thermometers, and their readings have been compared with differences in output, accident and sickness. There appears to be an optimum range or zone within fairly wide limits of tolerance where most workers feel comfortable, not too warm or too cool. This zone ranges from about 60° to 75° on the ordinary thermometer for sedentary work and light work,[1] but is probably lower on heavy labour. This is a range of temperature that appears to yield lowest accident-rates, and absence from sickness and highest output. Above that range, at 77°, accidents in a munition works were found 23 per cent greater, and below that range, at 52°, 35 per cent greater than at a temperature of 67°[2]. In

[1]Industrial Health Research Board Report 76.
[2]ibid. Report 19.

cotton weaving a maximum of output was found at temperatures of 72° to 75°.[1] Humidity of the air has also been found to raise human accidents and lower output, and in linen and cotton weaving there is thus a clash between conditions favourable to human efficiency and favourable to the warp-threads which are less apt to break when damp.

It is in coal mining that evidence about the effect of air conditions on accidents, output and sickness absence is most complete.[2] As the depth of the mine increases, temperature rises, and air is more stagnant; the accident rate rises, and rate of output falls. For instance, in parts of a mine with most air movement, seven and three-tenth minutes per hour were taken in rests as against twenty-two and two-fifths where air movement was least, and it took eight minutes to fill tubs as against nine and three-fifths. Analysing the sickness of over 33,000 miners Dr. Vernon and others found that a rise of 10° to 13° in temperature was associated with an increase of 63-74 per cent in sickness rates. This was attributed largely to the men getting chilled on the way home before they could change their damp clothes and indicated the need for pit-head baths.

Like air, lighting conditions may lead to inefficient labour because of extremes—darkness on the one hand, glare on the other, and some medium degree of light is likely to be the optimum for efficiency. Degrees of light can be measured in foot-candles, and it has been found from exact measurements of foot-candles and of units of output (e.g. number of tiles pressed, or output of compositors) that output is often increased and quality of work improved (particularly in fine work liable to strain the eyes) by stronger natural or artificial lighting. At two foot-candles printers' errors were found to be more than double what they were at twenty foot-candles of light.[3] Accidents increase when natural light fails, as at twilight before artificial light is switched on. Inefficiency arises here partly from the physical invisibility of objects, partly through the

[1]ibid. Reports 21, 37.
[2]ibid. Reports 39, 51.
[3]Joint Report Industrial Health Research Board and Illumination Research Committee 1926.

fatigue, eye-strain and other physiological effects upon the human factor straining to see these objects.

Labour efficiency often requires, however, a more complicated arrangement than merely strong light, namely a high concentration of light on the work in hand, like footlights on a play, together with an avoidance of shadow effects and a suffusion of general light all round, possibly by indirect lighting helped by light coloured walls. Where work is sedentary or at a fixed spot, this situation is easily produced and accidents may be as low if not lower at night than by day, but where work is peripatetic as in railway yards, concentration of light on work in hand is not so easy and accident rates are usually higher at night than by the natural light of day.

Noise has been defined by Professor Bartlett as "any sound treated as a nuisance," and hence there can be too much, but not too little of it. Degrees of noise are now measurable, and noise beyond a certain degree has been shown to diminish industrial output at least slightly. Weavers who were induced to plug their ears, obtained a work curve starting considerably higher than that of weavers with ears unplugged. This suggests that the initially low output of the normal work curve may be due to lack of practice in the sense of a difficulty of adaption each new day to unpleasant factory conditions. The worker gets used to them, it is true, but at a certain cost to output and to himself. Bartlett[1], indeed, considers that the harm noise chiefly inflicts is not externally measurable. The worker produces the same output, but at a greater internal effort to counteract the disturbance; and the more the work puts a demand on the higher mental processes, the more disturbing the noise is likely to be. Though not always measurable in output, noise may consciously or unconsciously deter workers from work. The high rates of lost time and of requests for transfer shown for the noisy departments in Table 10 may well be symptomatic.

§4 MOTION STUDY

Industries vary in the type of work and physical conditions they offer. Much industrial work involves physical danger,

[1]*The Problem of Noise.*

muscular and nervous strain, monotony, noise and unhealthy dust and air conditions, which diminish efficiency. But not all these physical conditions need be accepted and suffered as inevitable. Some of them may be altered to suit human needs and capacities and to ease the effort and reduce the danger involved in a given output. The "Safety First" movement, for instance, and the less publicized but persistent efforts of factory inspectors to fence dangerous machinery, have greatly reduced the accidents of given occupations; and research in occupational medicine has kept down occupational diseases.

The most hopeful line of attack on such waste of man-power is motion study. In the widest conception analysis should be made not only of each existing job, but of alternative systems of "deployment" in splitting up and laying out the work of a group. Some factories and offices may not at present specialize their working force sufficiently, with consequent loss of the "improvements in the productive powers of labour" attributed by Adam Smith, in the first sentence of the *Wealth of Nations*, to the division of labour. In other factories and offices mass production may be overspecializing the jobs of workers with consequent boredom and loss of interest. In the narrower conception analysis is made of each existing job, and motion study aims at minimizing human effort per unit of output by changes in apparatus, in posture and above all in the movements of the industrial worker for performing that given job. Study of this sort formed part of the scientific management introduced by Frederick Taylor who called it hand-wisdom.

The design of apparatus used in industry often neglects the capacities of the worker. Taylor and his colleagues had to work out for themselves the most appropriate shovels for various types of material, or of mortar boxes and scaffolding for bricklaying. Apparatus, too, is not always made to fit the height or shape of workers nor to ensure economy of output. Costly breakages of crockery in tea-shops have been traced, for instance, to collision when washing-up with metal taps not protected by rubber. The consequent irritation of workers may reduce efficiency as much as the purely mechanical deficiencies of the apparatus.

Posture is important in itself and, in conjunction with

apparatus, determines the most efficient lay-out of the work. Gilbreth, for instance, "developed the exact position which each of the feet of the bricklayer should occupy with relation to the wall, the mortar box and the pile of bricks, and so made it unnecessary for him to take a step or two towards the pile of bricks and back again each time a brick is laid."[1]

As a result of experiments, several laws of posture and consequent design of apparatus seem to emerge. Fatigue and boredom are reduced by changing posture such as alternately sitting and standing, as well as by introducing variety in the work itself. In carrying loads by hand, it is least wasteful of effort to avoid displacing the body from its natural centre of gravity over the feet. By comparison with seven other methods of carrying exactly similar loads over the same distance, the milkmaid's yoke was found to involve least oxygen consumption and least increase of pulse rate, blood pressure and respiration over the lying down position. The most wasteful method was found the common practice of carrying a load on one hip. Such scientific discoveries result in practical instructions like this: "In wheeling loads in a barrow (arms hanging straight and the body erect) the downward pressure on the hands should be limited to fifteen pounds and the legs of the barrow should be long enough to minimize the effort of raising it to the wheeling position."[2]

As its name implies, motion study has contributed most to easing effort, in studying the actual movements of the worker. Some movements may be found entirely unnecessary. Of those retained, the elements analysed are speed, path, persistence and regularity of repetition. Speed can be stop-watched, as described in Chapter VIII, and forms, with the elimination of movements, the main element in time-study for setting wage rates. Path, persistence and regularity are more complex, though here again certain scientific laws emerge.

The path of a motion may be disclosed photographically either by a slow "movie" or by a "still" exposed while a light attached to the worker's hands or tools traces out their movement by white streaks. The most efficient workers are found

[1]Taylor, *Principles of Scientific Management*, 1913, pp. 77-8.
[2]Industrial Health Research Board, Reports 29 and 50.

often to prefer circular to direct paths between two points. Though longer distances are traversed, these movements give a swing and make use of existing momentum, which a direct path, often reversing directions and jagged in appearance, would lose. When swing is combined with evenness or regularity of motion, a rhythm is set up which, as in marching, dancing or rowing, carries the performer along almost unconsciously without nervous strain or boredom.

The degree of regularity in repeating industrial operations and parts of operations has been closely measured. Efficient workers repeated certain operations at fast speeds almost as regularly as they could tap with a finger,[1] but it was observed that they took considerable rests (partly camouflaged) after a run of, say, twenty minutes. It is probable that the fast and regular repetition necessary for rhythm could not persist without fatigue, but as rests were taken, the machine-work curve, as described in §1, did not fall. Authorized rest pauses without worry about camouflage are thus indicated as a relief from the fast rhythmical runs, and as part of motion planning. The basis for rhythm however is movements that can proceed smoothly, without stoppages to look over material and tools, or to inspect progress. "Music while you work" will help output if the work can thus run smoothly and unconsciously, but it may be a hindrance to quality and economy of output. If any thought and care has to be exercised, the noise may prevent concentration.

When the motions found by experiment to yield rhythm and involve least effort have been taught to new workers, their output is usually higher than that of more experienced workers using the traditional methods. With the increasing pace of the industrial revolution new machines and new operations are introduced into factories more and more frequently. This adds to the opportunities of testing more efficient methods of work at the outset. Motion study thus links up with training discussed in Chapter IX as part of the plan for labour efficiency.

---

[1]Florence, *Economics of Fatigue and Unrest*, pp. 244-248.

CHAPTER VI

SOCIAL RELATIONSHIPS IN EMPLOYMENT

§1 THE SOCIAL PATTERN OF INDUSTRY

THE position of the average worker in much of modern industry may be summed up as dominated by four "Rs": repetition, routine, red-tape and risk.

The repetitive nature of work in manufacturing, with its attendant feelings of monotony, has already been considered under physical conditions, and changes in conditions that would reduce or prevent monotony are suggested in a number of chapters.[1] Routine and red-tape on the other hand, are social conditions largely due to the size of the economic organization. They tend to give the worker a feeling of being just a cog in the machine. The small working group still predominates in agriculture, in building and in shop keeping. But in most lines of manufacturing the trend is towards larger and larger factories. While men still hanker after the homelike atmosphere of a small face-to-face group or gang, where everyone is called by his Christian name, economic forces are pushing them into huge agglomerations where not even family names are known—everyone is just a check-number, as in a prison. Instead of the boss (or, to use an English word, the gaffer) passing the time of day with him, there is a board of directors miles away—probably in London—issuing paper orders that gradually percolate through a regular hierarchy of officials of various ranks, from general manager to foreman, before they reach the man actually on the job. It is not an easy situation for human nature to stand.

Routine is a physical matter of working regular hours, under regular conditions, and according to regular technical practices necessary if a large organization is to work efficiently as one body. With growing division of labour, mechanization, standardization and mass-production, labour must (to be efficient)

[1]See pp. 29, 60, 76-7, 130.

work where the machines are, side by side, and simultaneously as a team. There can be little "outwork" in one's own home when one likes. Hence the galling necessity of time schedules and of clocking in and out, and the worry over absenteeism.

Though much of the red-tape is unnecessary to efficiency, there is here also an underlying necessity; not the technical economy of the large-scale physical plant but the organizational economy of the large-scale unit of control—the firm, company or combine. There are undoubtedly savings in large-scale buying and selling, finance, planning and co-ordination. Red-tape in the sense of centralized and systematic ordering of operations cannot be eliminated any more than routine; but recent observations and experiments, shortly to be described, show that certain excesses of both can be avoided with gain rather than loss to efficiency. Neither a large factory nor a large firm need be impersonalized institutions with uniform patterns of behaviour, held together merely by forms and formal procedure. Feelings of frustration and the sense of being a cog, though always a danger in modern industry, are a danger that can be guarded against.

The risk element in the worker's position is his liability to dismissal at short notice and thus (unless he can get another job) to unemployment. Plans for preventing unemployment are set forth in Chapters XI and XII. Here it is sufficient to point to the feeling of insecurity which pervades the working classes and its effect on output and efficiency. This feeling was built up during the period before the First World War when there was little unemployment insurance, and in the period between the world wars when, though there was insurance against it, unemployment was seldom less than 10 per cent. Once built up, the feeling of insecurity persists in spite of the official assurance of a full employment policy. Those in employment still feel that if they do any more work or if machines are introduced, it would merely be putting more persons out of work—"taking" as they feel, "the bread out of the mouths of others." Ways of thinking will persist after all cause for them has gone. Most workers to-day are thus still haunted by the bogy of unemployment. A fundamental problem in preventing low output is to assure the workers full and stable employment

TABLE 11: CHART OF THE WORKERS' SOCIAL ENVIRONMENT.

Underlying technical and organizational causes.	Aspect to the worker.	Workers' reactions and feelings	Ways and means of prevention or remedy
Mechanization and Division of Labour	*Repetition*	Monotony	Incentives; Rest Pauses; Vocational Selection (see Chapters IV, VIII, IX)
Large scale { Operating Unit (Factories)	*Routine*	Cog in the Machine	Supervision; Identification of Interests; Welfare Work; Personnel Consultation (see §3).
Controlling Unit (Firms)	*Red-Tape*	Frustration	Democratic Participation; Two-way Information and Control (see §4).
Industrial fluctuation and technical change	*Risk*	Insecurity and Restriction of Output	Full Employment Policy; Unemployment Benefit; (see Chapters XII and XIV).

and thus to produce a sense of security and confidence, and yet (for the sake of incentive) not to assure them the same terms for inefficient as for efficient work.

Methods of preventing insecurity of employment or, short of that, of palliating unemployment by monetary benefits are discussed in Chapters XII and XIV. Meanwhile, Table 11 can be drawn up to chart the psychological and social position of the worker and to steer the discussion in this chapter. To the worker the technical characteristics of modern industry given in the first column, appear in the aspect of a pattern of repetition, routine, red-tape and risk. This pattern evokes certain reactions and feelings tending to inefficiency, which can be prevented by various ways and means. Until recently these reactions were unknown territory but an industrial sociology is being developed, mainly in America, the preliminary results of which are reported in the next section.

§2 Recent Industrial Sociology

During and just after the First World War economists and industrial physiologists had made due note of the social conditions confronting the workers in the modern factory, the variety of incentives offered and yet the restriction of output and failure (in many groups) to work up to capacity.[1] Not until 1927, however, was any large scale intensive observation made of the actual reactions and attitudes of workers, when Dr. Elton Mayo of Harvard University was invited to the Western Electric works at Hawthorne, a suburb of Chicago. The main method he used was to observe in detail the output, waste time, behaviour and conversation of small groups of workers. One group consisted of five girls sitting at a bench assembling standardized parts of the telephone, called relays. The inquiry was originally planned to discover the effects of a shortened working day with rest pauses and refreshments and better illumination, but though output rose from the isolated test group such physical factors were soon found relatively unimportant at least within wide limits of tolerance. A return with the consent of the workers to the original forty-eight-hour working

[1]*See* especially H. M. Vernon, *Industrial Fatigue and Efficiency*, pp. 126 ff. Florence, *Economics of Fatigue and Unrest*, pp. 219, 223, 240.

week did not affect output. Since there was never any question of working longer than forty-eight hours and the work was not heavy, those results do not conflict with the British war-time evidence given in Chapter IV, but it was interesting that the same hours should, at the start of the experiment, produce less output than they did later on.

Mayo explains that the individual workers became a team and this team gave itself wholeheartedly and spontaneously to co-operation. The increase in the output since the time when the workers were in a normal factory department was attributed primarily to the release from the workers' own restrictive traditions and from ordinary discipline and harsh impersonal supervision. As a result of this interpretation an interview procedure was adopted throughout the factory by which it was hoped to find out what was "on the worker's mind" and to free that mind from fear of oppression. The history of the relay assemblers illustrates the impact upon labour of the four "Rs" in its modern social environment. The assemblers found the repetition work and routine boring, they responded to the cutting of red-tape by increased output, but later failed to keep up that increase when the risk of unemployment threatened them like any other workers.

Observation of the behaviour of another group of workers on telephones, the bank-wirers, brought out further elements in labour's social environment. As Professor Mayo puts it himself[1], "the ordinary conception of management-worker relation, as existing between company officials, on the one hand, and an unspecified number of individuals, on the other, is utterly mistaken. Management, in any continuously successful plant, is not related to single workers but always to working groups. In every department that continues to operate, the workers have—whether aware of it or not—formed themselves into a group with appropriate customs, duties, routines, even rituals; and management succeeds (or fails) in proportion as it is accepted without reservation by the group as authority and leader." Here are some of the rules of etiquette forming part of the unofficial code of behaviour of the Hawthorne bank-wirers, rules, many of which clearly run counter to the manage-

[1]*Social Problems of an Industrial Organization* (1945), pp. 81-2.

ment's view of efficiency and lead straight to restriction of output.

(i) You should not turn out too much work. If you do you are a "rate-buster."

(ii) You should not turn out too little work. If you do you are a "chiseler."

(iii) You should not tell a supervisor anything that will react to the detriment of an associate. If you do, you are a "squealer."

(iv) You should not attempt to maintain social distance or act officious. If you are an inspector, for example, you should not act like one.

To those who have been "through the mill" of an English public school this social situation will not appear improbable or unfamiliar. All these rules are there observed; though the names given to their violators may be different. Rate-busters have been called swots, chiselers slackers, squealers sneaks. Americans apparently had no name for (iv) but familiar English slang is swank. This code in the American factory and English public schools was as inviolate as primitive rituals; to break it was taboo—simply not done, or if done the violation would lead to social ostracism. British inquiries into the social relationships within the factory have not been so thorough but also supply an inkling of the importance of unofficial group "codes" running counter to efficiency.[1] Workers are related to their work less than is supposed by the cash-nexus—or by interest in the work itself (the hobby-nexus)—, more by a gang-nexus or status-nexus. His group with its code of conduct, and his standing in the factory hierarchy is equally important to the worker as his wage or his work. During the war, for instance, workers in many groups continued to regard the employer as the traditional enemy and as soon as the Axis powers appeared bound to lose anyway, "the impulse to have a round with the traditional enemy" crept up again.[2] The wage is often appreciated

[1] Industrial Health Research Board, Report 69; Hall & Locke, *Incentives and Contentment*; Mass Observation, *People in Production, War Factory*; Marie Jahoda, "Some Socio-Psychological Problems of Factory Life," *British Journal of Psychology*, January 1941.

[2] Mass Observation, *People in Production* (1942), p. 333.

less as providing income, than as a badge of rank. The higher the wage the higher the position or status. This attitude often lies behind insistence on maintaining the wage-structure as between different grades.

An attitude of the working group irrespective (and even disrespectful) of business policy, and anxiety about personal status illustrates the persistent importance of primitive patterns of social relationships, even in the midst of the latest devices of engineering science. It throws us back to considerations of elementary political science such as democracy and discipline and the organization and processes of ruling. The following sections outline the problems in social and political relationship —in routine and red-tape—presented by large-scale factory operations and the large unit of industrial control.

§3 SUPERVISION, DISCIPLINE AND WELFARE

Where large numbers of workers are employed, it is not possible for the employer to keep his eye on the work of all his men. The larger the firm the more ranks must come between employers (often a board of directors) and operatives; and the ranks immediately above the operatives in the factory will have to concentrate on the task of actual supervision. These ranks, equivalent to the non-commissioned officers of the army, the sergeants and the corporals, are in industry the foremen and "charge-hands."

The duties expected of the foremen vary in different factories according to the degree of specialization resulting from the introduction of personnel, planning or time-study departments. In factories of the old school, the foreman was supposed to hire (and fire) men, train them, set their wage-rates, keep the machines running and the material flowing through, look to the quality and quantity of output, as well as handing on orders and sending back records. So varied were the foreman's jobs that Frederick Taylor proposed to split up his work into eight parts and to give each to a separate "functional" foreman. This policy has not been generally adopted, since it would destroy unity of command in the department. An operative would too often not know to which of his eight foremen to bring his difficulty. The modern practice is for the foreman to be relieved of planning, of wage-setting, of hiring and of maintenance of plant by central offices, but still to retain the interpretation and execution of the manager's orders "on the floor" itself, and the efficient co-ordination of men and machines to perform the allotted work up to standard.

Where many machines are in use the foreman must usually be a skilled mechanic. But his work is clearly just as much concerned with the human as the mechanical factor. Ideally, he should be the captain of a team of willing workers, and occasionally such a foreman is found inspiring and "integrating" his co-workers. But there are other types, described by Hall and Locke in their *Incentives and Contentment*; the bully and the bureaucratic official, on the one hand; the mere "persuader" on the other. The operative will react accordingly and many of the psychological problem cases investigated at the Hawthorne Works regarded their foreman as an "ogre," constantly watching and ready to pounce on any mistake. The reaction of the typical operative is, however, not usually suppressed fear of the "sack." His everyday attitude is shown by the use of the pronoun "they" to describe management and foreman, thus failing to identify himself with the factory as a whole and taking up a position of irresponsibility toward the policy of his unit. This failure in *esprit de corps*, disclosed in the Hawthorne inquiry, if coupled with lack of interest in the work itself is likely to check efficiency. The majority of workers, thanks to some sense of duty, some traditional group pattern, or their own natural pace (see Chapter II, §3), will no doubt carry on at a certain "satisfactory enough" rate of output and absenteeism. But to keep the efficiency of the *whole* team up to standard, discipline rules must involve stimuli to work and deterrents from slacking applicable to every individual worker. To put it in concrete terms, a few individual "problem" workers are all the time impervious to the general attitude against "doing too little work" or unattached to the duty-nexus; and some further individuals impervious some of the time. National man-power needs require that *all* capable persons be employed efficiently.

The old stimulus for keeping up standards of discipline in industry was punishment by dismissal and the consequent chance of unemployment if the dismissed worker could not find another job. If full employment is to be successfully inaugurated, a substitute for this device may have to be found, as was the case in Russia. "In the absence of full employment, when an army of labour reserves is available, labour discipline is automatically enforced by the fear of losing one's job. Full employment may contribute in weakening labour discipline. The Soviet experience was that the abolition of unemployment led to a deterioration of labour discipline, such as excessive labour turn-over, rising absenteeism, late arrivals to work, idleness in working time, carelessly performed work, etc. To combat these consequences of full employment it proved necessary to resort to controlling the movement of labour by labour books, the obligation to give a month's notice, etc., and to penalizing absenteeism, lateness and other infringements of labour discipline, by such measures as reprimands, transfer to less highly paid work, dismissal entailing the loss of benefits acquired during employment, etc."[1]

To reduce the need for such disciplinary punishment, positive rewards must be planned—the carrot substituted for the stick. Piece-wages are an automatic reward for output, and hourly time-wages for attendance and punctuality. These money payments will be considered in the next chapter. There are, however, non-financial incentives to discipline, too. In Russia titles such as that of "Exemplary Worker," "Hero of Socialist Toil"; medals such as that for "Prowess in Labour"; and the organization of "shock brigades" and "socialist emulation" between whole works in record-breaking productivity were all aimed at preventing restriction of output and reducing absenteeism and turnover. These incentives culminated in the Stakhanov movement which encouraged the worker himself to think out new technical methods of production and new "motion studies" to reduce costs of production.

These plans will not achieve success unless the labourer identifies himself with the organization in which he works. If he thinks he is being exploited by capitalism, a medal or title for hard work will only be looked upon with suspicion, if not derision, by the worker. Devices such as these are useless

[1]Baykov, *Soviet Economic System*, p. 361.

if planted on hostile or even neutral soil. The worker must feel himself a partisan. This was realized in Russia where, in addition to the liquidation of private capitalism, the trade unions were in 1930 called upon to carry out official industrial plans rather than their traditional policy of protecting the workers' interests against the employer. They were to bring the working masses to participate in factory administration.[1]

Under capitalism and even in the nationalized industries of countries mainly capitalist, identification and participation is difficult to achieve. Welfare work may be conceived as an attempt to secure greater identification of the worker with the organization in which he works, making him feel more attached and "at home" in his workplace. It can be defined as the offer by the employer of amenities and facilities over and above those necessary for production. Amenities include physical conditions more congenial to the worker than Factory Acts command; facilities include meals in canteens, recreation, education, medical treatment, pensions, legal advice, social clubs. Many of the welfare facilities are conducive to the health, safety and efficiency of the worker and attract and "attach" him. First-aid stations by efficient treatment reduce days lost by accidents, and pensions should reduce labour turnover. Safety propaganda and especially safety committees make the worker feel a participant in the prevention of accidents. His interests are identified with that of the firm and the routine to which all are subject in the factory is qualified and a more personal basis introduced.

Until recently, the atmosphere associated with welfare work was, however, patriarchal. This comes out clearly in the house organs or factory magazines published with numerous photographs of employees like a family album. To-day a more suitable approach is typified in personnel management (see p. 186) and the personal interview advocated by Elton Mayo. A personnel counsellor can interview or be interviewed by any worker. Such an interview may give emotional release to the worker who fears dismissal or is haunted in his dreams by his foreman. And, without violating the confidence of the worker, the interview gives the management some idea of the causes

[1]Op. cit., p. 224.

underlying the attitude of workers toward production, their state of mind or "morale." The interviewer, however, must be carefully selected and trained. He must be tactful and yet take what he hears with plenty of salt and without being shocked.

Intelligent supervision, welfare work and facilities for individual consultation may all help to get the worker identified with his unit and at home with his work. To achieve all-out efficiency, however, without reservations and restriction, identification with the controlling organization must be supported by some participation in control itself.

§4 DEMOCRATIC PARTICIPATION IN CONTROL

After the First World War, a cry arose for control of industry by the worker. In its extreme form the cry has now subsided, possibly because the meaning of control is more closely analysed.[1] The ultimate core of control is the determination of amounts and sorts of production, of the price to be charged and of the necessary investment in equipment and stock; the appointment of efficient managers to existing posts; and the organization of new posts where necessary. Both the ultimate control, usually called administration or direction, and the higher management of an industry is a skilled professional job in itself, requiring knowledge of markets and consumers' demands and needs, and general training and experience, which neither operatives nor trade union leaders necessarily possess. Trade unions, as described later, have exerted a controlling influence on wages, hours of work and other employment conditions over whole industries and occupations. But for the main purpose of industry—production—factories must be managed by specialized, trained and experienced professionals appointed for their efficiency by those who can judge and compare efficiency.

Efficiency of management is likely to create confidence if not a certain pride in the workers, and may serve as an example in efficiency all round. Yet the process of specialization, however necessary to national production, does run the danger of separating the industrial community into two worlds, with an iron curtain between the management hemisphere concerned with efficiency, and the proletarian hemisphere isolated from

[1] *See* Florence, *The Logic of Industrial Organization*, Chap. IV, §9.

thoughts of efficiency, and concentrating instead on grievances and a sense of injustice about orders imposed upon it from above and seldom explained. Large scale industry cannot be efficiently run by elected representatives of the workers, yet there is no reason why the workers should not have explanations of the orders as well as the bare orders; why they should not contribute detailed skill and knowledge and experience they possess by means of suggestions for technical improvements; why the part their work plays in the whole organization should not be made intelligible; or why they should not be able to state their grievances directly (as well as their suggestions for improvements) by joint consultation in Works Councils or Production Committees within the factory or firm. Possibly more decentralization of control might bring responsibility home to the worker. Dubreuil, for instance, advocated (and the Bata Works practised) small departmental accounting units to fit the range of the visual field of the average worker. Devices such as these might make both for efficiency and democracy.

Democracy is not just a matter of everyone recording a vote or attending meetings. Its essence has been distilled in three affirmations: that each individual counts and has a life to live; that each may contribute in determining policy and those controlling policy should be sensitive to the views of all; and that out of conflicting opinions a decision can be reached by discussion.[1] Applied to industrial production democracy demands in particular more two-way traffic in discussion—orders and explanation going along the ranks while information, grievances and opinion comes back by some agreed procedure so that the individual worker may feel he counts. In this way he will learn not only to identify himself with the whole organization and its interest in efficiency but to participate.

This social participation reinforcing the incentive and attractive power of individual supervision, welfare and counselling, can be fitted into the democratic organization of the whole craft or industry built up by the trade unions. As their name implies trade unions are organized trade by trade, that is by craft or industry, not by factories or firms; their control of working conditions in various trades as a whole is discussed in

[1]*See especially* Lord Lindsay, *The Essentials of Democracy*.

Chapter XIII. Trade unions, however, may, and do, link up with single industrial organizations through their representation on Works Councils and Production Committees and by their appointment of shop stewards, factory by factory.

The process of democratic participation must develop the discussion stage whereby participants can be co-ordinated in the sense that they adjust their views reciprocally one to another. Modern thought on large-scale administration points to the necessity of the co-ordination of specialists rather than the exercise of sheer authority. As Mary Follet points out in her *Dynamic Administration*, there must be co-ordination by direct contact of all the responsible people in the early stages of discussion and as a continuing process. Clearly the representatives of labour are among the specialists responsible for labour conditions. The background "climate" and the use of these principles of participation in dissipating labour suspicion cannot be better illustrated than in the issue, which to-day overclouds perhaps all others, of profits versus wages. It is true that under the *laissez faire* capitalist system profit could be, and was, made by reducing the share of the product going to the workers, but now with powerful trade unions, Wages Joint and Industrial Councils safeguarding wages it is not so much the sharing process that keeps down wages and standards of living but rather the total amount of product to be shared. The worker now tends to get a small slice of cake in the form of wages not because someone else has a bigger slice in the form of profits or dividends, but because the whole cake is small. Yet, with scientific invention continually extending the possibilities of productivity per man, the total size of the cake should enlarge if the process were not obstructed by a sort of "hangover" from the days when the employer (in the absence of trade unions and State legislation) could eat into his workers' slices.

The quickest cure for the "hang-over" which continues to restrict output is to convince labour that the profits from sale of output left after payment of wages and salaries are not excessive in the sense of greater than necessary for securing the supply of capital required. This can only be achieved by giving more information on the trading accounts to the representatives of labour and by putting before them the financial results of alternative policies. In finance as in control generally, labour must be co-ordinated by direct contact from the start and as a continuous routine procedure.

CHAPTER VII

THE AMOUNT OF THE WAGE

§1 THE WAGE AND WORKING CAPACITY

THE harnessing of the human factor to the needs of society was described in Chapter II as a process of making the worker capable and willing to be efficient at his job and capable and willing to move to other jobs if these were more in demand or needed. In a free society with a minimum of coercion wages help in this process more, probably, than any other industrial condition. Wages are spent on food and other necessities for life and efficiency, and thus nourish the worker and make him capable for work; they can be exchanged for whatever consumable goods and services are available for the price of the wage and thus make the workers willing to earn them; and differences between the wages in different industries and occupations can hold workers in given jobs or attract them from one job to another, as society's need or the consumer's demand requires.

The mobilizing effect of wages in making workers stay in a job or move from one job to another will be taken up in §3. The "nutritive" and incentive effects of the amount of the wage in a given job will be taken up in this and the following sections.

Considerable, though fragmentary, research has been undertaken on the relation of wages and capacity to work, and the line of reasoning may well get lost in a welter of facts unless the argument is explicitly stated. The present argument will run as follows: (i) the bulk of workers' incomes comes from wages and is spent on necessaries to life and efficiency; (ii) the total necessary food can be calculated in terms of calories and vitamins, and allowance made for the minimum of other necessaries; (iii) calculated on this theoretical basis, the income of workers has not always proved sufficient, as death rates confirm; (iv) and the extent of the actual insufficiency of income is greater than the theoretical, since wages are not in fact always spent on necessaries first; (v) this insufficiency of income was in the years before the last war due not to low wages of an average family, but either to abnormally large families or to unemployment. Hence the need for a policy of family allowances and full employment.

(i) Successive surveys into workers' family budgets have shown that while the income consists almost entirely of earnings by way of wages, expenditure is mainly on food, housing, clothing and other things necessary to life and efficiency. The proportions of total expenditure spent on these necessaries[1] are given in Table 12 for British workers' budgets in 1904 and

TABLE 12: PERCENTAGE OF EXPENDITURE SPENT ON NECESSARIES

Groups of Expenditure	Weights[2] used in Cost of Living Index 1914-47 (Based on 1904 Budgets)	Ministry of Labour Workers' Budgets 1937-8[3]	Civil Service Budgets 1938-9
Rent and Rates ..	16	13	12
Fuel	8	7.5	6
Food	60	40	24
Clothing	12	9.5	9
Other Items ..	4	30	49
	100	100	100

1937-8 and for the budgets of middle-class civil servants in 1938-9. In 1904 the average real earnings of a worker were (as we shall see) considerably lower than in 1937-38. Comparison of the three columns confirms conclusions reached by a wide series of budget inquiries (first initiated by Christian Engel) that where wages and incomes are comparatively low, a greater

[1]Arranged as in P.E.P. Broadsheet No. 220.
[2]*See* below, p. 209, footnote.
[3]After allowing for price changes 1938-47, used as weights for cost-of-living index commencing 1947.

proportion of the income is spent on necessities than where incomes are higher. Engel's law that the proportion of expenditure spent on food falls as total expenditure increases has also in Germany and America been found true of housing and of fuel and light. Items which increase *out* of proportion upwards as total income and expenditure increases include entertainment, holidays, keeping servants and also savings. Clearly the lower the income the more the recipient is forced to confine himself to necessaries. If his income is below a certain point he will fail to get the total amount of food, fuel, houseroom and clothing necessary for his health and efficiency.

(ii) The necessary food for living and for working efficiency consists of three "major constituents," proteins, carbohydrates and fats. The heat and energy value of a given weight of each of these can be expressed in calories. While mere living requires food with a basic calorie content depending on age and sex, the calorie content of food required for work varies greatly with the work's heaviness. Authorities[1] estimate that a boy of seven requires 2,100, a boy of eleven or a girl of thirteen 2,800 calories a day, a moderately active woman 2,900, a moderately active man 3,500, but a very active man 4,500. The total calorie requirement of a family that wages have to feed thus depends not only on the number and work of its members, but on its composition; women and children are, for purposes of totalling, counted as fractions of a (moderately working) adult male "eating unit." A standard family is usually taken that will maintain the future population, consisting of man, wife and three children (eventually to replace the parents and to make up for persons not reproducing). A family composed of a (moderately working) man, his wife, a girl of thirteen, and boys of eleven and seven requires 14,100 calories a day, equal to that of 4.03 male eating units.

Food should supply not only the energy measurable in calories necessary for various types of persons and work, but also specific vitamins A, B, C, D, etc, for the prevention of specific deficiency diseases, and minerals particularly necessary

[1] e.g., Stiebeling modified by Wokes, *Food, the Deciding Factor* (1941), p. 16 and footnote.

for growing children. The price of the mixed diet that is thus called for as a minimum for the health and efficiency of a standard family can be, and has been, calculated from time to time. When added to the price of minimum standards in housing, clothing, fuel, etc., it forms one of the bases for the minimum wages determined by official Trade Boards or Wages Councils.

(iii) In nineteenth-century Britain efficiency often suffered directly from the underfeeding of the workers. Lord Brassey in his *Work and Wages* tells how his father when building railways and drainage systems found that workers when paid higher wages produced a greater output per given amount of wage, and thus established an economy of high wages by lowering labour cost. Though partly due to increasing the capacity of labour, this economy may also have been due to the higher wages stimulating the employer to manage and equip his labour more efficiently, so as to get equivalent output. This past experience of employers is supported by statistics of comparative disability and death rates in different occupations. Where wages were generally low, workers with the lowest earnings have more sickness than workers with earnings less low,[1] and on the whole the more poorly paid occupations have distinctly higher death rates than the higher paid. The Registrar-General classifies occupations into five income classes. The second and fourth are intermediate respectively between the first, the professional class and the third, the skilled class; and between the third and the fifth or unskilled class with the lowest wages. The comparative death rates in the homogeneous first, third and fifth classes may be given here.

Salient points are the wide gap between the death rates of males of the first and fifth classes, a gap which is, however, gradually closing; and the gaps in the class death rates of the wives of these workers in 1930-32—still wider than their husbands' in the same years. These comparisons support precisely the contention that the amount of wages and incomes affect health. The difference in the incomes of different classes was diminishing but was still very wide in 1930-32. Other factors, besides the amount of wages received, occur in the

[1] *See* Florence, *Economics of Fatigue and Unrest*, pp. 342-6.

COMPARATIVE STANDARDIZED MORTALITY RATES AT AGES
TWENTY TO SIXTY-FIVE

Social Class	Percentage of Average Rate, All Classes		
	Occupied Males		Wives
	1921-3	*1930-2*	*1930-2*
(i) Professional	82	90	81
(iii) Skilled ..	94	97	99
(v) Unskilled ..	124	111	113

differences between men's death rates in different occupations,
such as exposure to unhealthy types of work, but these factors
do not apply to the wives. They all have much the same housework hazards, yet show even wider income-class differences in
death rates than their husbands. These differences in death
rates may thus be attributed substantially to differences in total
expenditure on food and necessaries (including housing and
medical service).

(iv) A series of social surveys, and also trends in wages and
prices, detailed in Chapter XIV, show that real wages (wages
in terms of cost of living) have risen and that the proportion
of workers insufficiently provided for has fallen since 1899.
Yet the comparatively high death rates among the unskilled
and their wives in 1930-2 still tells the tale of actual poverty.
A worker may be "provided" with sufficient wages to enable
his family to avoid falling below the primary poverty line, but
it does not follow that he or his wife will actually spend those
wages in the manner most likely to conduce to health and
efficiency. A distinction has been drawn between primary or
unavoidable poverty and secondary or actual poverty. The
social surveys conducted at various times and places, such as
York in 1936 and Bristol in 1937, when unemployment was not
excessive, showed the proportion of families in primary poverty
to be only between 6 and 7 per cent. The high proportion of
families left above the primary poverty line did not, however,
mark the proportion of workers in fact sufficiently fed, clothed
and housed for full working capacity.

In calculating primary poverty, the expenditure allowed for subsistence is strictly controlled according to the analysis (page 91) of what is necessary. At 1936 prices and taking rent as 9s. 6d., Rowntree allowed 40s. 1d. for the bare subsistence minimum (and 53s. 0d. for the human needs) of a York man, wife and three children, which (according to the cost of living index) would be equivalent to 55s. 3d. (and 73s.) at 1946 prices. The average earnings per man given in Table 14 (page 106) are considerably higher than these minimum standards, but not all families with incomes above these standards do, in fact, spend enough on necessaries for bare subsistence or on human needs; a further proportion of families will be in "secondary" poverty where on Rowntree's definition "earnings would be sufficient for the maintenance of merely physical efficiency were it not that some portion of it is absorbed by other expenditure either useful or wasteful." Sir John Orr estimated in 1936 that nearly half the population were not securing adequate amounts of certain types of foodstuffs. The differences between this large proportion and the percentages (between 6 and 7 per cent) of families in primary poverty marks the degree of malnutrition due to unwise spending of income. Consumers cannot all be expected to be 100 per cent wise and hence the wages paid must allow a certain leeway over and above necessary expenditure, if, at ordinary levels of consumer intelligence, they are to ensure feeding, housing and clothing adequate for health and working efficiency.

Primary poverty is insufficient income, secondary poverty is income insufficiently wisely spent, to ensure physical health and efficiency. Poverty in both forms existed up to the outbreak of war in 1939, and the causes of primary poverty were analysed in detail. Between 1920 and 1939 it was chiefly unemployment rather than low earnings that pulled families below the primary poverty line. The proportion in poverty in the different areas surveyed varied mainly with the rate of unemployment, not with the rate of wages or earnings. Apart from unemployment, the families earning below the bare minimum for their health and efficiency were those where (owing to death, sickness or accident) there was no adult male breadwinner, or where there was one breadwinner with too many non-earning dependants.

D

The Bristol survey found, for instance, that though the proportion in primary poverty was only 6.5 per cent for *all* families sampled, the proportion was 51.3 per cent for families with more than four children. At Kingstanding[1] there was a relentless correlation of the proportion in primary poverty and number of children. Among families with one child, 3 per cent were in primary poverty; among families with two children, 11 per cent; among families with three children, 27 per cent; with four children 55 per cent; with five children 60 per cent; and finally among families with six or more children 82 per cent. Since every family must pass through the stage where the children are all dependants, families of more than four children are very likely to find themselves below the poverty line early in their career, when the children most need care. The health and capacity of a large proportion of workers is thus threatened to-day mainly by unemployment and large families.

§2 THE AMOUNT OF THE WAGE AS AN INCENTIVE TO WORK

Variations in the amount paid in wages affects not only capacity to work efficiently, but also willingness. Downward revision of money wages, even though the cost of living may be falling in proportion, causes resentment, and, as illustrated by the deflation of 1920-6, large-scale strikes. But a rise in wage rates may not result in a correspondingly strong incentive. The relation of wages and willingness to work is not direct, and is only gradually becoming recognized. It turns upon two psychological facts. The first is that most people visualize in their minds what wages can buy; the second that in this vision classes of people have certain similar living standards which condition their buying habits.

Visualizing beyond money wages to the things money will buy, I have called the transpecuniary incentive. The average worker is not a miser or a hoarder and he will want more wages only if there are more purchasable goods and services within his reach. If rationing or high prices restrict purchases, the transpecuniary incentive will be weak. Workers "value wages for what they will buy, and if no leisure is provided for buying

[1]A Birmingham housing estate. *See* Soutar, Wilkins and Florence, *Nutrition and Size of Family*, 1942.

desired objects or enjoying their possession, or if no facilities
for pleasure are afforded by the locality in which they live and
work, or again if every effort of the worker to raise his standard
of life by . . . indulging in some luxury produces an outcry,
then employers cannot expect the wages they pay to offer any
great incentive to workers."[1]

The standard of living is used here in the sense of some
ideal but practical budget of consumption and use of leisure
that the worker has in mind. This standard may be well above,
near, or the same as the actual mode of living of his family. If
the worker does not set his standard above his actual mode of
living, and does not want more income to change that mode, an
increase of hourly rates of pay will merely result in fewer
hours being worked and an increase of rates of pay per piece
merely in fewer pieces being made. Increases in wages will,
in short, be the opposite of an incentive. This case does not
appear exceptional in Britain, as the observations of Dr. H. M.
Vernon in shipbuilding and coal-mining testify. Among the
shipbuilding crafts he found that lost time increased with
increases in the scale of pay, and fell with a decrease in the
scale. For instance, in the case of drillers time-keeping was
poor in 1900 to 1902 when pay was fairly good, whilst it was
good from 1904 to 1909 when pay was low, then it gradually
got worse again as pay improved and it was specially bad in
1912 to 1913 when pay was at its maximum.[2] British coal-
miners' wage rates, and therefore the earnings they could make,
were severely reduced between 1924-6 and 1927-8. Comparing
10,000 underground workers in the same pits in the two
periods Dr. Vernon[3] found absenteeism greatly reduced by the
change. The reduction in wage rates meant that the possible
earnings of the coal face worker fell 32 per cent. At the same
time their time lost by voluntary absenteeism fell to a half. The
other underground men were similarly affected, for when
their possible earnings fell 24 per cent their absenteeism from
voluntary causes fell 38 per cent.

This incentive to attendance associated with a fall in wage

[1]Florence, *Economics of Fatigue and Unrest*, 1924, p. 257.
[2]Vernon, *Industrial Fatigue and Efficiency*, pp. 151-2.
[3]Industrial Health Research Board, Report 62, p. 33.

rates rather than a rise indicates that the worker is driven to work by encroachments on a low fixed standard of living, rather than encouraged by the possibilities of rising to a more ambitious standard. Conservatism of this sort obviously sets up obstacles to an increased output per man, which can partly be overcome by accustoming the worker to new types of goods and services. An ambitious housing policy would set up demands for additional furniture and fittings and a general rise in the whole mode of living which only increased earnings can satisfy. Another incentive to earn more wages are holidays which take families out of their routine manner of life. The output of workers on piece wages is often found higher in the weeks preceding a holiday. The more ambitious the holiday and the clearer it is visualized, the more earnings workers will presumably strive for beforehand, to spend on that holiday.

The chance of earning money in order to save, seems less of an incentive to a higher output, except for the relatively few families of a stern cast of thought. Till recently economists (being mainly of that cast of thought) considered most saving to be a deliberate act. It is now recognized that saving among the majority of rich and poor is an automatic consequence of income being larger than the routine mode of living and "propensity to consume," rather than a deliberate plan. But here again, if workers can visualize some actual commodity to save for, such as the purchase of a house or of a small business, a "transpecuniary" incentive will be set up. In circumstances where the mobility between social classes is freer and workers see no limit to the possible rise in their worldly position, this incentive will be the stronger; more work will be done for a greater amount of wages and promotion is likely to be sought to grades paying higher wages or salaries.

§3 Wages as Attractives to Mobility

Economics is largely concerned with the problems of distributing the supply of national resources over the various demands made upon them. Man-power is one, now probably the most important, of these resources. The first chapter described recent changes in the distribution of labour in Great Britain between certain key industries. To effect the required distribution more or less compulsory direction was used during the war; but wages policy is the mechanism easiest to operate in a free society at peace.

Different industries, occupations or grades have certain inherent circumstances peculiar to themselves which cannot readily be altered. Adam Smith, in his *Wealth of Nations*,[1] mentioned five such circumstances "arising from the nature of the employments themselves," which "make up for a small pecuniary gain in some employments and counterbalance a great one in others: first, the agreeableness or disagreeableness of the employments themselves (further analysed into the ease and hardship, the cleanliness or dirtiness, the honourableness or dishonourableness of the employment); secondly, the easiness and cheapness, or the difficulty and expense of learning them; thirdly, the constancy or inconstancy of employment in them; fourthly, the small or great trust which must be reposed in those who exercise them; and fifthly, the probability or improbability of success in them."

Of these five circumstances, that of cost of learning and of "trust" can be put forward to explain the customary pattern of wage and salary differences between grades of workers within any one industry. Normally every industry contains within itself a traditional structure of basic wage rates whereby the skilled craftsmen of various grades receives perhaps 20 to 60 per cent more than an unskilled labourer, besides still higher percentages of the wage rates of women, boys and girls. Table 13 presents a typical wage structure agreed upon by workers and employers in 1946. On the whole the differences between grades have been closing in; they were still wider in 1938 than 1946. The differences between men's and women's wages will be discussed later. The wage "differential" between skilled and unskilled men is usually explained as due to the longer experience required for the higher grades when they are recruited by up-grading, or as due to the time the skilled man originally had to spend as an apprentice at a low remuneration. Similarly the supervisor, administrator and professional man gets higher pay than the skilled worker because of his still longer schooling and professional training and also perhaps the trust reposed

[1] Book i, Chapter X.

TABLE 13: EXAMPLE OF AN AGREED WAGE STRUCTURE
INDUSTRIAL AND STAFF CANTEENS, 1946[1]

Basic Wages Rates Per Week

Grades.	Men s. d.	Women s. d.
Porters	70 0	—
Canteen Attendants	—	50 0
Cashiers	—	53 0
Assistant Cooks	85 0	57 6
Cooks	97 0	65 0
Head Cooks	110 0	80 0
Supervisors, Stewards	110s. to 140s.	80s. to 110s.

47-Hour Week, 44 hours guaranteed. Meals and work-clothes provided—10s. more if not.

in him. Apart from certain inborn qualities needed for such work which may be relatively scarce, the cost and length of training cuts out the majority of boys and girls whose parents cannot afford the fees or the loss of earnings involved while learning. Owing to their limited supply—if for no other reason —those who get a training can obtain higher pay.

The other circumstances, however, have not hitherto acted upon wages as clearly as Adam Smith supposed. Higher paid jobs are on the whole more interesting and agreeable in themselves (quite apart from the salary) than poorly paid jobs; are more constant (i.e., less liable to unemployment) and hold more promise of success than poorly paid jobs. What Marshall called the strange and paradoxical result arises that the dirtiness of some occupations is a cause of the lowness of the wages earned in them. The reason for this discrepancy of fact from the theory of counterbalancing advantages is mainly immobility between social classes resulting in non-competing groups. Dirty work was low paid in the opinion of Marshall writing in the eighteen-nineties because there were many people "unfit for any but the

[1]Source: Ministry of Labour, *Time Rates of Wages and Hours of Labour at August* 1946.

lowest grade of work" competing for the work, "the influence of (whose) surroundings has prepared many of them to regard the dirtiness of an occupation as an evil of but minor importance."[1] Thus low standards breed low standards and the theory has to be modified to read that *within the same social class*, certain circumstances are liable to make some employments less attractive and to require higher wages in compensation.

Circumstances other than the five mentioned by Adam Smith now also appear important as attractives or deterrents. A strong attractive to which recent inquiries point is companionship. Factories, for instance, attract girls as compared with domestic service in households that only employ a cook-general; and as the Hawthorne experiment showed workers are particular as to the people in their working group. The desire to have and keep friends and to stay a member of a small group —the gang-nexus—is also powerful in holding workers to their "home town" and making them less willing to move geographically.

Mobility is increasing between social classes, and there is to-day in Britain no longer any large class indifferent to dirtiness. Adam Smith's theory (allowing for the discovery of a few additional repellent and attractive circumstances) has therefore a wider actual application than in his own time. Disagreeableness in the form of heavy, exposed and dirty work fosters scarcity of miners, farm workers and foundrymen. Agreeableness, in the form of honour and respectability, results in an abundance of salaried white-collar workers, often earning less than a manual worker paid by the piece. Indeed, honour and respectability now appear among the strongest attractives. Adam Smith pointed out "that the most detestable of all employments, that of public executioner, is in proportion to the quantity of the work done better paid than any common trade whatever," and modern social research has shown the importance in the worker's mind of his "status." He values independent status, and thus "small" shopkeeping on his own attracts him beyond the meagre income and in spite of a heavy labour turnover by bankruptcy. If he cannot be independent, the worker wants a status superior to some other dependant,

[1] *Principles of Economics*, VI, iii, §8.

or the chance of promotion to foreman or chargehand. The fact that in many industries the craftsman is dying out and that the only test of status among operatives is the relative wage itself, adds a psychological, non-financial importance to the wage structure.

Given social mobility competition is supposed in theory to equalize the wage of people engaged in trades requiring equal skill and effort. Marshall[1], warning against a crude comparison of money wages, brings into the theory Adam Smith's non-financial counterbalancing circumstances beside the cash-nexus, in his notion of "net advantages." "The true reward which an occupation offers to labour has to be calculated by deducting the money value of all its disadvantages from that of all its advantages (including the wages); and we may describe this true reward as the net advantages of the occupation."

Marshall's lead might be followed up by an analysis or balance-sheet of a job's attractions and deterrents, its human assets and liabilities, many of which are measurable. Unemployment and death rates are known for all the different industries, and sickness, disability and accident rates, too, for many of them. Cost of learning can be assessed and (as shown in Chapters IV and V) relative degrees of fatigue and boredom. On the asset side the prospects as against blind alleys can be estimated from the grade-structure of an industry and the ratio of employers and manager to operatives; sociability as against loneliness, by direct observation. Casting up a balance would then give a basis for a counterbalancing wage policy to preserve the *status quo*, or to move workers from one industry to another. Domestic servants in small households, for instance, might still be found insufficiently compensated for loneliness and lack of status and prospects; lorry drivers (enjoying an interesting and sociable life on the road) found with no counter-balance in wages relatively low.

The problem hitherto wrestled with has been that of adjusting wages fairly to counterbalance different circumstances of different jobs affecting their attractiveness to supplies of labour. There is an immediate difficulty in that downward adjustment of wages will be strongly resisted. Two, more fundamental,

[1] *Principles of Economics*, Book II, iv, 2.

considerations cannot be ignored, though they may (and do) appear to many people to lead to "unfair" wages. The first consideration still concerns the supply of labour. Chapter I pointed out that the inherent abilities of men vary. If the type of ability that society needs or demands is scarce, its wages and net advantages may have to be raised above other wages however unfair it may seem, so as to ensure that workers with that type of ability are recruited where they are needed. Before justifying too sharp a difference between the true reward of different jobs, however, we must be certain that all artificial barriers to social mobility have been removed, and that it is really a natural scarcity that is being overcome.

The second consideration concerns the demand for labour. The demands and needs of a community are not of equal urgency and do not remain fixed. In war-time the urgent demand is for implements of war and for fighting men; in peace-time demand turns back toward work and workers that will make up the war-time deficit in durable goods such as houses or clothes, and with continuing peace, new standards of living develop requiring a change in the distribution of man-power. To adjust the labour supply to the relative urgency of demands and needs, and to effect the necessary changes in distribution of labour from the *status quo*, wage policy is again the instrument most ready to hand, though other circumstances such as length of training, amenities and hours of work may also be adjusted. In theory urgency of demand for a product or service will involve higher prices being offered on the market, hence higher profits for the producers, hence ability to pay higher wages to more workers.[1]

Do differences in the actual wages or earnings of industries in fact reflect differences and changes in urgency of demand? Clearly if the demand changes in direction (as away from the metals required by war toward the building and clothing required in peace) particularly high wages should be offered to reverse the flow of labour. Table 13 gave basic wage rates for a normal week in different grades within one industry, but the financial attraction we here want to study is that exercised by

[1] In technical terms, the "marginal" productivity of extra workers will, with higher prices of products, be worth higher wages.

whole industries and may consist in the total actually earned not the wage rate. Earnings differ from stipulated wage rates since they are affected by the hours worked (work in overtime hours is paid extra), and by the pieces produced on piece wages (piece-rate workers normally earn more than others). Table 14 is therefore presented comparing the larger industrial groups both by total earnings per worker and (as an approach to wage rates) by hourly earnings.

Comparing the six large groups of manufacturing industries, including building, given in Table 14[1], the differences are much wider in average earnings for all workers than in total or hourly earnings per man. The highest average earnings *per man* were in metals, the lowest in textiles. The difference was only 20 per cent for weekly and 21 per cent for hourly earnings whereas the difference between minimum and maximum average weekly earnings for *all* workers in these six industry groups

TABLE 14: AVERAGE EARNINGS PER WORKER IN THE LARGE INDUSTRY GROUPS, OCTOBER, 1946

INDUSTRY GROUP (In order of weekly earnings, all workers)	WEEKLY EARNINGS		HOURLY EARNINGS Adult men only
	All workers	Adult men only	
	s. d.	*s. d.*	*s. d.*
Metal Engineering and	114 4	132 9	2 9.2
Shipbuilding	(max.)	(max.)	(max.)
Transport and Storage	110 4	115 2	2 3.6
Building	103 0	110 7	2 5.2
Food, Drink, Tobacco	87 10	112 6	2 3.7
Textiles	78 3	110 0	2 3.4
		(min.)	(min.)
Clothing	70 0	114 9	2 6.9
	(min.)		
% Difference of Maximum over Minimum	63%	20%	21%
All Industries	101 0	120 9	2 6.4

[1]*Ministry of Labour Gazette*, April 1947, p. 108. Industry Groups employing less than 500,000 excluded.

was 63 per cent of the minimum. This wide divergence is mainly due to the different sex and age structure of different industries—industries employing larger proportions of women or young persons have lower average earnings. When the average earnings of the same class (like adult men in Table 14) are considered, equality appears among the different groups of industries, whatever the relative urgency or change in urgency of their work may be. Equality of earnings per man would be approached still nearer if similar grades of skill within each industry were separately compared and piece-rate earnings (where effort is normally greater) separated from time-rate earnings. In fact, as theory suggested, the money wage of similar classes of workers and grades requiring similar skill and effort seems to tend to equality. Recent changes in wage rates have accentuated this tendency because the extractive industries of agriculture and mining, relatively low paid grade for grade before 1939, have since then advanced their wage rates faster than other industries. The relative advance may be due to a recognition of the urgency of the need for food and coal and the disagreeableness of farming and mining. Until further changes are recorded, however, the evidence is that the dynamic function of wages in adjusting scarce labour supply to urgent national demands in particular industries takes second place to the static idea of the "fairness" of equality in money wages (or perhaps net advantages) of similar grades whatever the industry.

§4 SUMMARY

The amount of the wage paid to labour has four broad functions to perform in the economic system. Wages must be adequate to conduce to health and working capacity in the working force and also, perhaps, the reproduction of the population; they must be an incentive to efficiency; they must be "fair" in counterbalancing the disadvantages of some occupations and industries; and in conjunction with other advantages they must attract workers where workers are demanded or needed by society and overcome any natural or temporary scarcity. How far does the actual wage system of any country fulfil these functions? In Britain the lowest real wages are gradually rising to ensure working capacity, but there is a danger that rising rates of pay per hour or per piece with stationary conventional standards of living will be a deterrent rather than an incentive to more hours or pieces. With more social mobility wages are becoming "fairer" in counterbalancing the disadvantages of occupations and grades, but owing to remaining privileges, and to high cost of training (in fees and in loss of possible earnings while under training) social mobility is still incomplete, and in the absence of any centrally planned wage policy there is insufficient adjustment to changes in the needs of society. In consequence, pockets of relatively unwanted immobile labour and peaks of unsatisfied demands appear and are likely to reappear.

When obstacles to mobility of labour such as exclusive schools, professional and trade union practices and unnecessary length and cost of training are swept away, it is the wage or salary differences that must mainly be relied upon to adjust the supply of labour to the demand. This is as true under State planning as capitalist enterprise. In Russia indeed, it appears that differences in wages, and in what wages can buy, are deliberately fostered to obtain the planned distribution of labour, and attention will probably have to be increasingly paid in Western countries to the effect of equality and differences in the amount of wages paid. It will be shown in Part IV (where alternative forms of control are canvassed) that in Britain and America to-day the fixing of wages is largely in the control of the employers and the workers *in each industry.* The result of this collective bargaining sectionally for each industry, is not calculated to lead to a co-ordinated system of wages. Labour will not necessarily be distributed so as to reflect the needs or demands of the community as a whole.

CHAPTER VIII

METHODS OF WAGE PAYMENT

§1 COMPARATIVE EFFICIENCY OF TIME AND OF PIECE RATES

Two opposite poles of wage payment are payment according to time worked and payment according to pieces made. Direct observation has shown, as might be expected, that more pieces are made per day when wages are paid by the piece than by the hour. In 1915 I recorded the output of two shifts of seventeen girls drilling fuses, in two consecutive weeks, one before and the other immediately after changing from time to a piece wage.[1] The output on the day shift was 24 per cent, the output on the night shift 40 per cent higher on piece than when on time rate. Higher rates of output on piece rates are, indeed, generally admitted, and further advantages accrue both to employer and worker, as a result of piece rates which may be symmetrically arranged thus:

Advantages of Piece Rates

To Employer:	*To Worker:*
Greater output	Greater earnings
Labour cost easy to calculate for each piece	Fair reward for personal effort
Less supervision required for quantity of output	More independence acquired

Yet probably less than half of all industrial jobs are paid by piece rates, and it may well be asked why, if piece rates are more productive and advantageous to both parties, more industrial jobs are not paid in this way. The answer is that piece rates are often either impossible; or less efficient all-round; or dangerous to "morale."

On many jobs piece rates are impossible, because there are

[1]Florence, *Economics of Fatigue and Unrest*, pp. 253-4.

no uniform pieces, or no pieces at all. There is much work like that of watchmen, policemen, transport workers, agriculturists and shop-keepers where no measurable pieces are produced. Even if work does produce pieces, the number of pieces made may have no relation to the effort involved. Though mining is generally paid by the piece, miners may strike a "difficult place" where coal is harder to get, and then be paid by time, just as a shop assistant may strike a difficult customer. Certainly a bus driver's load does not depend on his own efforts or even his conductor's.

Quantity of output is not the only test of efficiency. Piece rates often result in a speeding up that scamps the quality of work. Piece rates in certain processes have been known to yield such a high percentage of spoiled work that the employer has deliberately changed to a time wage. Speeding up may also affect the all-round efficiency of the worker, causing a high accident and absentee rate, not to speak of a lower output rate in the long run. The Industrial Health Research Board[1] found a drop in the middle of the output curve for each spell when time wages were paid, though piece wages usually lead to a fall at the end. The monotony effect attributed to time wages may thus lose no more work output on a long day than the fatigue attributable to piece wage speeds.

That morale may suffer under piece rates has been brought out by further investigations of the Industrial Health Research Board. One group of girls were found when on piece wages to have three times the number of quarrels and complaints, than when on time wages.[2] There will be more jealousy and a loss of team spirit when each worker is striving for his own higher earnings. Even when earnings were higher on individual piece rates, a lower proportion of women workers paid on those rates have been found satisfied with the wage received, than the proportion that were satisfied on time wage.[3] "You can rely on it" was a frequent reason given for preferring the time wage. Workers may question the fairness of the piece rates themselves

[1]Report 77.

[2]Report 69, p. 20. Morale may be defined simply as an attitude of a group favourable to efficiency.

[3]Report 88, p. 10.

(we shall return to this later); almost half the women on piece rates were dissatisfied, mainly because of alleged inequality in the rates of payment for similar types of work.

The case for piece rates is thus not a foregone conclusion; but the quantity of output per man which piece rates seem to stimulate is so much higher, that the cause of national efficiency calls for efforts to extend their use, particularly if precautions are taken to set the rates fairly.

Though many jobs will remain which cannot be paid by the piece, there are always, even under a time-rate system, certain indirect financial incentives to output. A worker may be promoted or demoted to grades earning a higher or lower time rate, or be discharged altogether if his output or attendance is not satisfactory. To be effective this action on the part of the employer involves the keeping of accurate records of workers' productivity and absenteeism. Many firms have found that such accurate records together with close supervision result in output as high as though paid by the piece. Usually a quota of output is set below which the worker must not fall, and there is careful scrutiny of results. The Industrial Health Research Board (Report 72) found that workers who are set a target figure or some other standard of attainment will improve in speed and accuracy, and will prolong their efforts, as against workers who have no set standard or who may adopt standards lower than those of which they are capable.

§2 COLLECTIVE PIECE WAGES AND PROFIT SHARING

In teamwork or wherever a large number of workers are engaged on a common task, output often cannot be attributed to each individual. In such a case a collective piece wage or bonus is frequently paid; the whole team or department receives a wage determined by the total output of pieces and this wage is then distributed among members of the team or department either equally, or on some pre-arranged system. The strength of the incentive appears to depend on the numbers of workers in the team or group. If a very large department is involved, incentive may be lost, since each individual worker will feel his work has little effect on the total output; but if the group is small enough to have a "face-to-face" relationship, the incentive may be intense because slacking is noticed by fellow members who will feel that their earnings are being reduced by the lower output.

Among women the proportion dissatisfied with their wages and with the actual rates set, has been found less on collective than on individual piece rates. Typical opinions were: "We've just gone on to group payment, and I prefer it to individual. Although the money is less, it has stopped all the bickering among the girls." "I prefer the group rate because there is no favouritism, but sometimes a slacker causes trouble."[1]

Profit sharing may be referred to here, since it is in the nature of a collective wage to the employees, varying with the market value of the output of the whole factory. Schemes of profit sharing (called co-partnership if the employees take up shares) have been reviewed year after year in the Ministry of Labour *Gazette*, and it is worth quoting from the last review before the recent war.[2]

"The number of profit-sharing schemes (apart from those in co-operative societies) known to have been in operation at the end of 1910 was 125. From this date until 1929 there was a fairly continuous increase in the number of schemes operating. Since the end of 1929 the number of schemes in operation has shown a decline each year." From the time when schemes were first recorded 411 were known in 1939 to have failed. In 1930 there were 341 schemes covering 214,000 employees, in 1938 only 261 schemes but covering about the same number.

Since the total of industrial employees runs into millions, it may be asked why such schemes were failing and were falling in number, and why the number of workers included was stationary at such a low proportion of the possible total. The answer has already been partly given. The "collectivity" is probably too large for incentive effects; the individual worker cannot see how his particular effort will influence the output of a whole factory. To which the possibility is added that profit or loss may be due, not to the manual workers at all, but to some success or mistake in the sales or purchasing department or among other brain workers. A further explana-

[1]Industrial Health Research Board, Report 88, p. 13.
[2]*Labour Gazette*, August 1939.

tion is that the actual share of the profits comes long after the work it pays for and forms on the average a very small part of the normal wage income. The Ministry of Labour *Gazette* analysing all schemes where data were available found that in the ten years 1929 to 1938, the average percentage addition profit shares made to earnings ranged only between 4.8 to 6.1. To be an incentive to efficiency then, schemes for a collective wage on output, or a collective share in profits, require a small homogeneous collectivity and a fairly large and immediate addition relative to ordinary earnings. In a small face-to-face group whose earnings consist entirely in collective piece wages, incentives to high output and low absenteeism and turnover are likely to be strong.

§3 COMPARATIVE EFFICIENCY OF VARIETIES OF INDIVIDUAL PIECE RATE

The piece rates discussed thus far have been mainly so-called straight rates, where the wages earned collectively or individually are in strict proportion to the output. Variations, however, can be introduced particularly in individual piece rates. The wages may be arranged to vary progressively more than in proportion to output, or degressively less than in proportion. Where a worker is operating or tending a costly machine, the profit from his output is *greater per piece* the more pieces he makes, for the overhead cost of the machine is constant whatever the output. If he makes twice the normal output, his output is more profitable than that of two workers put together, each making a normal output, since their work involves depreciation and maintenance costs of two machines instead of one. The employer can therefore afford to pay the double-speed worker more than the two workers together, and the exponents of scientific management, from its founder Frederick Taylor onward, have been perfectly logical in advocating progressive piece-rate systems, or at least lump sums added to straight piece rates when a certain number of pieces were achieved.

However in British engineering it is the opposite method of a degressive wage that appears to be more usual under systems such as the Halsey or Rowan "premium bonus." The more pieces a worker turns out, the more he gets in aggregate, but the less he gets per piece. The precise formulae used are given in §4 and can be found in multitudinous text books, but the results on efficiency are seldom chronicled. In my own experience both in Britain and America these degressive systems of piece work are associated with deliberate restriction of output.

The evidence for restriction of output is (1) the repetition of the same output figure for different persons, though these persons should (as shown in Chapter I) vary in their capacity; (2) the repetition of the same output figure day after day, though with changes in physical conditions, the output on different days should vary; (3) the ability of the same workers to produce at a higher rate of output, shown after machine breakdowns, so as to make up the uniformly repeated daily output; (4) the candid statement of workers that there is a limit agreed upon, often with a name attached to it such as the "stint" or "doggie."

The links connecting degressive piece rates with restriction of output are psychologically clear enough and do not necessarily involve Trade Union "defensive tactics." Much the same links connect restriction with progressive taxation, for a rate of tax increasing progressively with higher income means a degressively increasing net income. If wage earners understand the formula of degression of wages (or net income) they may quite reasonably decide that after a certain output the diminishing return is not worth the effort. If wage earners don't understand the often complicated formula, they tend to ask the foreman what precise output will satisfy the management, and leave it at that. Thus a social tradition of stereotyped output grows up, or if already there (as described in Chapter VII) is reinforced.

If degressive piece-rate systems are associated with restriction of output, why, it may be asked, are they adopted in preference to straight piece rates; and why are progressive systems of piece rates not more frequently tried, since progressive systems, justified by the savings in overhead from high output, usually result in higher output per man than do straight piece rates?

The reason usually given is the fear of the worker that if he goes all-out and makes large earnings, his rate will then be "nibbled" or cut. Such a cut or the fear of it will, of course, be a deterrent to output and invite deliberate restriction, and is rightly condemned from the standpoint of efficiency. Yet few of the legion of critics of rate-cutting realize the employers' dilemma. Where there is any error in setting piece rates for different jobs such that workers with similar skill and effort can earn more wages on one job than another, then if the employer cuts rates, he checks output on that job. If he does not cut rates one worker may earn perhaps half as much again as another with the same skill and effort. This inequality usually results in envy, suspicion of favouritism, and lower morale in the sense of a feeling of unfairness inimical to efficiency. The only solution of this dilemma is to be more careful about setting the original piece rates. Degressive piece rates are frequently adopted because (however unfair the standard output required as between different jobs) the workers of whom too little output is required cannot make very much greater earnings by higher outputs than those of whom too much is required. If straight and especially progressive piece rates are adopted the divergence in earnings may be very great indeed, unless the day's work is set really fairly as between jobs. Degressive rates yield earnings on a given increase of output somewhere between the earnings on straight piece rates and on time wages. For their operation without loss of morale exact estimation of a fair output is not so essential; but to get efficiency without loss of morale from straight or progressive piece rates, the setting of the piece rate must be closely and laboriously studied.

§4 THE SETTING OF PIECE RATES

Setting piece wages involves three main steps: (1) finding a basic fair day's work for (2) a basic fair day's wage, and (3) formulating what wages (compared to the basic wage) deviations from the fair day's work shall get. Anyone familiar with economic theory might suppose that the wage would follow from the value of the work or "productivity" of the wage-earner, but in practice, the two steps are reversed. What is first in the mind of both employer and employee in their bargaining, is the idea of a fair day's wage for men or women of various grades of skill, or for boys or girls—and it is here we must begin.

(1) A fair wage usually means one hallowed by tradition and convention, and this tradition has normally taken some account of the circumstances described in the preceding chapter. A higher rate of wage will be paid to grades of workers who have had to undergo apprenticeship or long experience, or incur other costs of training, and whose work perhaps is disagreeable or involves trust and responsibility. But the degree of compensation for disadvantages is in most industries far from exact, and may lag behind the march of the industrial revolution.

Many modern employers are trying by so-called job-analysis or job-evaluation to make the process of aligning wages fairly to correspond with the disadvantages of the work, more scientific and less traditional. In one scheme for instance, high points are given for the precise length of the learning period and experience required by the job; for responsibility in connection with material and equipment; for heavy or dangerous work; and for work needing special precision, dexterity or mechanical ability, or work that is particularly complex. These points are added up and the higher the total of points, the higher will be the differential or "lead" of the fair wage for that job over that of other jobs. A whole structure of different wage and salary grades is thus built up by conscious thought and analysis, which it is hoped will appeal to people as compensating them fairly for the different circumstances of the jobs they are engaged upon.

(2) The fair day's wage for any job once found and agreed upon, a fair day's quantity of output in the job must be ascertained. The fair wage can then be divided by this fair output (in number of pieces) to yield a fair piece rate. If a fair day's wage for a given grade is taken to be 18s., and thirty-six pieces arrived at as a fair day's work, the basic piece rate will be 18s. ÷ 36, or 6d. per piece. But how exactly is the fair day's output arrived at? With the advent of scientific management, factory practice has developed rapidly since the day when the fair day's work on any job was merely estimated. The standard

task for a job is now arrived at either "synthetically" by calculation from known elements such as the machine speeds and feeds technically involved, and by comparing it with other jobs already studied; or directly by time study of the job itself. Time study has quite a literature devoted to it, but the main steps can be stated briefly.

The first step is to select the worker or workers and the time when and during which the study is to be made; the second is to time the several parts of the operation as it is repeatedly performed; the third (connected with the motion study referred to in Chapter V) to expurgate waste motions and unnecessary parts of the operation; the fourth, to compare the timing in the various repetitions of the job and (usually) to add up the fastest times for each of the correct motions, into an expurgated "ideal" total time; and finally to make the ideal a humanly possible standard of achievement by adding a delay or fatigue allowance, usually a percentage of the ideal time varying from 15 to 30 per cent, according to the type of job. The Bedaux system has acquired a certain notoriety but it is not unique and is only one variety of piece-rate setting, involving a time-study which happens to clothe the fatigue allowance in a picturesque terminology of "B" units. These units contain a fraction of a minute of work and a remaining fraction of a minute of rest, the fractions varying, according to the nature of the strain.

The standard time for a job which is the objective of the Bedaux and other time-study methods (and of most of the estimating, calculating and comparing that is resorted to) is some feasible task beyond the average actual performance. To be confronted with such a challenge, like the proverbial carrot in front of the donkey, undoubtedly provides incentive; but for long-run efficiency the question is whether the task set may not, in fact, often overstrain labour. The answer lies in the selection of the worker and the methods of calculating the fatigue allowance. Earlier practice selected the best worker only[1] but modern practice is to time-study any "good" worker, first "rating" him as, say, an eighty, seventy or sixty-five minutes-

[1]For criticism of the unscientific nature of the procedure see Florence, *Economics of Fatigue and Unrest*, pp. 91-5.

an-hour man and to make allowance for the average worker accordingly. This method, though more fair, makes it clearer than ever that human judgment enters into the calculation. A "good" time-study man will undoubtedly make well-judged ratings; but who can rate the rater?

The exact allowance by which the standard time is built up from the "ideal" time, to allow for the fatigue or strain of different types of work, has not (in spite of claims to be scientific) been the subject of much published scientific discussion. In fact, to justify the high fees demanded, many time-study consultants are inclined to put the ideal too high, and the fatigue allowance too low, and to forecast an output higher than their methods can really achieve. The consequent speed-up required from labour has frequently brought on strikes, and in any case made time study unpopular. Though present methods of determining the fair standard output are still in most factories crude, a few firms get workers' representatives to co-operate in the selection of the experimental conditions; they broaden the basis of time setting by studying several workers and co-ordinating results.

(3) In working out the wages which deviations from the standard output shall earn, the terms of the formulae are those very notions of a fair day's or hour's work, and of a fair wage, that have just been discussed. If the time allowed as fair or standard for a piece of work is called TA and the fair rate of wage for the grade of labour W, then the formulae deal mainly with the earnings of a worker when the time he takes (TT) is faster than the mere "fair" rate of work, that is when he saves TA-TT time out of the "fair" time allowed.

Under the Halsey system the worker is paid a "premium bonus" of half the fair wage for all time saved ($=$TA-TT) in addition to the fair wage rate for the time taken ($=$TT). The Halsey formula is therefore: Earnings$=$W$\times$TT$+\frac{1}{2}$W (TA-TT). To take an extreme example, if the fair time allowed is nine hours, the fair wages 2s. an hour, and the worker actually takes three hours, then his earnings for the three hours are (2s.$\times$3)$+$(1s.$\times$6)$=$12s. He took a third of the supposedly fair time, trebled the rate of work and got for the three hours 12s.— that is, 4s. instead of 2s. an hour. In short, *trebling* the rate of output results in *twice* the rate of pay—clearly a degressive piece rate. Under a rather more complicated system, devised by Rowan, the worker is paid, in addition to the fair wage for the time taken, a premium bonus equal to the proportion of the time allowed as fair which he saves out of the time taken. The Rowan formula is therefore: Earnings$=$W$\times$TT$+$ W$\times$TT $\left(\dfrac{(\text{TA}-\text{TT})}{\text{TA}}\right)$. If the same example is taken as before, the earnings for three hours work are $(2s.\times3)+(2s.\times3\times\frac{8}{8})$ $=$10s., or 3s. 4d. the hour. In short, trebling the rate of output results in one and two-third times the rate of pay—still more degressive for these high speeds than the Halsey system. However fast he works, a worker cannot under the Rowan system ever make more than double his basic wage.

Formulae based on a fair day's wage and a fair day's work can also be used to build up progressive wage systems. In this case the fair wage rate is increased for time saved or pieces made over and above the fair rate, either by a lump bonus (as under Gantt's task and bonus system) or by continuously increasing the rate per piece as total output increases (as under Taylor's "differential" wage system).

§5 THE COMPOSITE WAGE SYSTEM

The various methods of wage payment just described are not necessarily exclusive one of another. In fact most modern piece-rate systems allow for a minimum or basic time wage as a cushion in case the worker is not able to produce enough output to earn a living wage; and the same worker may be paid at a straight, or a progressive, or a degressive wage rate, according to the level of his output. A logical system (if it were not too complicated) would be to pay a time rate at the lower range of output, then, as output increased, to pay at a straight proportionate rate, then (encouraging still higher output which would reduce overhead charges) to pay at a progressive rate, but (putting a flexible limit on over-exertion) to pay for the highest range of output at a degressive rate. In addition, the whole time or piece rate system (or combination of both) may vary automatically from time to time on a sliding-scale, sliding either with a cost-of-living index number measuring change from a base period in the prices of a few key articles (grouped and weighted according to their importance in budgets of expenditure); or sliding with the price of the product, as measuring the market value of the worker's services.

Wages systems are complex, and complicated in different ways for different industries, often because they are the result of a long history of bargaining between employers and employed organized in associations and trade unions. It is this collective bargaining that has implemented and given precise value to the notions of a fair wage for different grades of workers; but collective bargaining has not succeeded for every industry in implementing the notion of a fair day's work. Changes in technique involved in the industrial revolution have often proved too fast, and too complicated for wage adjustment. If a new machine which makes a given output easier for the worker is introduced every few years, workers on that machine should have their standard fair day's task of pieces increased relatively to workers on the old machines. In the cotton industry, certain piece lists agreed upon by employers and workers do, in fact, allow downward adjustment for increased speed on newer spinning machines.[1] But in other industries such as engineering, the fair day's task is determined unilaterally by time study under the employers' auspices. Apart from the appointment of a shop steward to represent them in supervising time study, all that workers have succeeded in getting recognized is that the earnings of an average worker on the unilaterally set piece rates shall bear some relation to the basic fair time rate for the grade of labour employed. Since output is normally higher on piece wages, piece rates are usually fixed to yield 25 to 30 per cent more earnings to an average worker than the basic time wage.

How complicated a modern wage system may be, can be judged from the many uses of the adjective "basic" applied to a wage, for all sorts of reasons. The basic wage may be (a) the

---

[1] In weaving, piece lists do not, however, pay fairly as between different jobs for the effort of shuttle-changing and repairing of warp breaks. See Cotton Manufacturing Commission, *Inquiry into Wages Arrangements*, 1948.

time rate on which are calculated the higher piece rate earnings due to higher output; or the basic wage may be (*b*) the wage on some key grade of work to which additions are made for grades of workers of greater skill; or the basic wage may be used (*c*) to calculate additions or bonuses by some formula: (i) for workers exceeding the fair or standard rate of work within their grade, or (ii) for different times (possibly under a sliding scale for cost of living) or (iii) for different places. A worker may thus get additions to the basic rate because he is on a piece, not a time, rate; in a specially skilled grade; particularly efficient within his grade; and/or because the cost of living has risen or is higher where he lives than elsewhere.

These additions, however arbitrary they may seem on the surface, are each connected with one of the three functions of the wage—attractive, conducive, incentive—that were stressed in the last chapter. Skill may be scarce and costly to acquire and skilled workers must be attracted or others stimulated to acquire skill by additional pay. Wages must keep workers and their families in health and must conduce to efficiency, they must rise (or fall) whenever the cost of living rises (or falls) and wherever living is particularly dear (or cheap). And finally wages must be an incentive to efficiency and must be higher for those working more intensively.

CHAPTER IX

SELECTION AND TRAINING OF
INDIVIDUAL WORKERS

§1 IMPORTANCE OF THE WORKER AND HIS HOME SITUATION
THE conditions likely to affect labour efficiency discussed in previous chapters were all conditions confronting a worker at his place of work. Efficiency, however, is the product of the worker's characteristics as well as those of the work place. With the same factory hours, type of work, physical and social conditions, and the same wage and method of wage payment, two different individual workers may yet show very different efficiency: one worker may be more efficient generally than another, or one may be more efficient in one line, the other in another line. Inherent quantitative and qualitative differences in the intelligence as well as the physical make-up of individuals were described in Chapter I and form the basis (together with the more obvious variations between workers in attainments due to education or experience) for now examining the selection and training of workers as further conditions likely to affect efficiency.

Referring back to Table 3 in Chapter II we now take as given the left-hand and middle column "conditions of the work place" and "conditions of the wage," and set out to find how differences and changes in the right-hand personal characteristics of the workers affect such objective tests of efficiency as output, absence, accidents and labour turnover. These characteristics may be innate, may be attained (as by training), or may be "concomitant," e..g, due to the home life of the workers. With every worker selected, the employer brings into his employment a human being with his "pack of troubles," and recent research has discovered by personal interviews or otherwise, how greatly home worries may affect efficiency. Social conditions outside the work place, such as housing, town-planning (affecting the distance workers have to

122

travel every day), the various affiliations of the worker, and the conditions which during the war had to be dealt with as "outside" welfare, will all influence output, absence, turnover, accident and morale generally. Conclusions of recent objective inquiries into these concomitant circumstances may be briefly considered, before proceeding to the innate characteristics and attainments of workers. The general factor determining conditions outside the factory is the degree of poverty, already discussed under the amount of the wage, but there are also specific home circumstances affecting efficiency not necessarily the result of the family income.

A worker may for the same rent live near his work place in, perhaps, a crowded district, or may move outward some distance for more elbow room inside and outside his house. With planned housing estates and the policy of segregating factory from residential zones, the actual trend has been outward, and travel to work has become a serious cost in time and money to many factory workers. Of twenty-two factories giving sufficient detail, Liepmann shows five where at least two-thirds of all workers spent a total of more than an hour travelling forth to work and back home each day.[1] Travel was mainly in rush hours and thus crowded and exhausting.

Comparison of larger and smaller cities discloses that residents of the larger incur considerably more cost in travelling to work than residents of the smaller. A random sample of householders in Worcester with a population of 60,000 has been compared with a sample from Birmingham with a population of a million.[2] In Worcester 75.5 per cent of chief male householders with fixed place of work went without cost, 22.5 per cent spent 5s. or under and only 2.0 per cent over 5s. per week. In Birmingham (excluding 11.0 per cent with no fixed place of work such as commercial travellers) only 45.1 per cent of principal wage-earners incurred no cost, 40.5 spent 5s. or under, 3.3 per cent spent over 5s. per week. In London, the London Passenger Transport Board estimated in 1939 that £15 per family per year, or 8 per cent of the average income of

[1] *The Journey to Work*, p. 164.
[2] Glaisyer, Brennan, Ritchie, and Florence. *County Town: A Civic Survey for the Planning of Worcester*, pp. 103-7.

working class families went in transport.[1] There is objective evidence of the effect of distance of home from work in the higher rates of labour turnover and of voluntary absence found among miners the farther they live from the pits,[2] and it can be surmised that workers on the margin of doubt whether to turn up at work, may be adversely influenced by the prospect of a long, tedious and expensive journey. The time and energy spent on travel is likely to lower output and raise accidents, and the cost to diminish the actual level of living. In the long run the remedy lies in the siting of factories and housing estates closer together and modifying the present degree of housing scatter insisted upon. In the short run, with factories and houses "given," distance of house from factory may only be controlled by selection of workers with homes more easily accessible.

Home conditions, other than distance from work, that are not mainly a result of wages are largely social and psychological. In the case of women, home difficulties of housework and shopping may interfere with attendance. Among single women on war work who had a high rate of sickness absence, it was found that nearly half had home difficulties; among those with low sickness absence, less than a quarter had such difficulties.[3] Young persons, particularly girls, have in some families to give up virtually all their earnings to their parents; if they are on piece-rates economic incentive to high output then disappears.

Leisure activities in sports, hobbies, clubs and social intercourse generally (or their absence) are both a cause and a symptom of degrees of contentment and efficiency; the very pattern of the family life itself may play a part in adjustment of individuals to factory life. One life may compensate psychologically for the other. For instance, foremen may strive too hard for success in the factory because of a lack of any relationships outside; for them the company is father, mother, society and State all rolled into one[4] and they are more likely to make excessive and distorted demands on their subordinates. In

[1]*Royal Commission on the Distribution of the Industrial Population*, p. 358.
[2]Industrial Health Research Board, Report 51, pp. 48-9.
[3]Industrial Health Research Board, Report 88, p. 34.
[4]Roethlisberger and Dickson, *Management and the Worker*, p. 372

short, workers are not selected out of a vacuum and in the scientific selection now to be described, the circumstances of their life outside the work place cannot be neglected.

§2 SCIENTIFIC GUIDANCE AND SELECTION

The wide variation of human beings in their characteristics, and of jobs in their requirements clearly make the selection of workers for work so as to fit one to the other a matter of national economy. Misfits are a waste of the nation's manpower resources. In the particular aptitudes required by different jobs, persons vary no less than in the general intelligence and the physical features discussed in Chapter I. There are at least five scales or categories important to industrial appointments, along which human beings vary: physical characters, general intelligence, special aptitudes, attainments and temperament.

No doubt the practised employer after looking at a man's record of attainment can, to some extent, size him up psychologically, as he can his height, without the aid of any scientific technique. But employers are not all practised in the art, and even to the most practised, shrewd and artful sizing up by eye has limits. A thorough selection should combine art and science.

If there are many candidates a rapid examination by eye, "giving the once over," sieves out those most obviously hopeless. But after that, thorough physiological and psychological examination of the screened candidates becomes worth while. Measurement and testing of all the five categories important to industry have been scientifically developed in programmes of vocational guidance and vocational selection. Guidance looks at the matter from the standpoint of the person (usually a child) and asks what are the jobs for which his characteristics are suited; selection looks at the same matter from the standpoint of the job, and tries to find persons suited to its requirements.

The English vocational guidance experiment that has been most thoroughly followed up in its industrial results is probably that of the City of Birmingham Education Committee. In Birmingham and under most English educational authorities there is for every child leaving elementary school a choice of

employment conference at which an official of the local education authority attends the school and interviews (often somewhat briefly) the child in the presence of the head or class
teacher and (if they wish to come) of the parent or parents.
Advice as to a suitable job is then given in the light of the
child's appearance, answers and school reports, and of the
demand for labour in the neighbourhood.

Against this background the city of Birmingham has for
some time carried on a research in more scientific vocational
guidance. By 1944, the careers of 603 children had been followed
up for four years. These children, otherwise in similar circumstances, were split into two groups; 281 received advice only
at a choice of employment conference, 322 were scientifically
tested as well. The tests were designed in the first place to
measure the children's general innate intelligence. The tests
devised by psychologists to discover this readily are usually of
the types illustrated in Table 15. The test can be given to a
whole group and a time limit assigned so as to measure quickness as well as accuracy. Usually the later questions of each
type are more difficult than the earlier. The marks obtained
rank children according to their mental age, and their mental
age divided by their physical age gives their "intelligence
quotient" or I.Q. A child marked twelve by results of the test
but physically only ten years of age would have an I.Q. of
120 per cent.

Controversy has arisen as to whether literary-minded
children and children who are smart, alert, and quick in the
uptake, but not fundamentally intelligent, are not over-marked,
and whether there is such a thing as "general" intelligence at
all. Clearly this type of test cannot be taken as final guidance
into industrial posts, and it is usually supplemented (as at
Birmingham) by special tests of performance ability (such as
jig-saw puzzles), of manual dexterity and of mechanical or
dressmaking ability. In Birmingham the children are also rated
by teachers trained in psychological method on the score of
qualities of temperament (personal qualities, and qualities
affecting their work and their relations with other people) and
on the score of their reaction to the tests, and of their ability in
school subjects.

TABLE 15: EXAMPLES FROM GENERAL INTELLIGENCE TESTS.

One example of each type of question from Verbal Intelligence Tests prepared by the National Institute of Industrial Psychology.

Type I. OPPOSITES (underline correct answer):
Strange, Peculiar.
SAME, OPPOSITE, UNKNOWN
50 such questions, 3 minutes.

Type II. ANALOGIES (underline missing word):
CLOTH is to TAILOR as WOOD is to
TREE, CARPENTER, SAW, TABLE.
25 such questions, 3 minutes.

Type III. MIXED SENTENCES (unmix and underline truth):
A twelve year are in there months.
TRUE, FALSE, UNKNOWN
30 such questions, 3 minutes.

Type IV. COMPLETING SENTENCES (underline word making best sense):

	skirts		necessary	
In winter days are short and it is	foolish			to turn on the
	lives		dangerous	
	wireless	night's		
the taps before the day's			work is done
	lights	week's		

Type V. REASONING:
The first train starts at 8 o'clock and after that they run every 20 minutes, and they all take half an hour. There is, however, another train starting at 8.30 which takes thirty-five minutes. One day a man, who usually arrived at his office just on time, was five minutes late. Which train did he catch?
8.0 8.20 8.30 8.40 9.0.

What was the subsequent career of the children guided by means of psychological tests and ratings, as against the children guided only by advice at the school conference? Among both groups some took jobs in accordance with the tests or advice, others did not. But while of the children merely advised at the conferences who took jobs in accordance with the guidance, 27 per cent stayed in the job four years, as many as 46 per cent of those tested who took jobs in accordance with test results stayed the four years in the job. This seems to show that tests are more successful in prediction than mere conference advice. The fate of children who did not act according to advice or test emphasizes this, and shows the rapidity of the labour turnover where jobs are taken against the results of the tests. Among children taking jobs against mere advice, 26 per cent stayed the four years in their first job, almost exactly the same proportion as among those accepting jobs in accordance with advice; but among children taking jobs against their test results 11 per cent remained the four years in their first job, only a quarter of the proportion (46 per cent.) among those accepting the test results.

A further check on the efficiency of the psychological tests as against mere advice is the degree to which jobs taken up successively approach the type originally recommended by the test or by guidance advice. Of the tested children followed up four years, 80 per cent began their careers in jobs in accordance with the test; the number increased to 95 per cent in such jobs at the end of the period. Of the children merely "advised" 63 per cent began in jobs in accordance with that advice, but only 42 per cent were in such jobs at the end of the four years.

In choosing their workers and staff, employers will thus find that the school system's vocational guidance tests will reduce their labour turnover and save time in trial and error before worker and job are suited. But a more direct approach is through vocational selection which takes the exact job the employer wishes to fill and devises tests to discover the most suitable worker. Tests are devised in all five categories; a physical examination; tests of general innate intelligence or mental alertness; tests of the special aptitude (which can be very precise if a thorough analysis is made of the job first); a record of attainment at school or in previous employment; and tests or ratings of temperament. Physical examination and records of attainment need no explanation. Innate intelligence does not develop further after the age of sixteen to eighteen and selection uses much the same tests as vocational guidance. But more must be said of the selection for special aptitudes and for the temperament required for specific vocations.

A rudimentary special aptitude test in the Birmingham experiment was given for mechanical and dressmaking ability, and among the more intelligent children, for clerical ability. Clearly such tests can be further specialized for specific jobs and have, in fact, been developed for salesmen, packers, chemical workers, bus, taxi and engine drivers, inspectors of industrial products and many other varieties of work. The test may be analogous to the job—reproducing it in miniature. Or the test may analyse out certain "key" characteristics— in the work of salesmen, for instance, quickness of repartee has been tested as an important ingredient; for packing, hand and eye co-ordination and estimation of size. Both analogous and analytic tests before being used on new workers are themselves usually tested on workers of known efficiency. If test marks differ from proved efficiency in the specific jobs for which they are designed, the tests are reshaped.

A suitable physique, general intelligence and special aptitude is not enough to qualify for a job. These abilities must be backed by a suitable temperament, personality or character. To begin with, if a worker has no energy or perseverance, external incentives may be useless; if he has great drive, initiative and inner incentive, external incentives may be unnecessary. Other temperamental qualities picked out by psychologists as important to industry are quickness and carefulness; self-confidence, aggressiveness, leadership; sympathy, sociability, co-operativeness, sensitiveness, discrimination. All these temperamental qualities are difficult to assess objectively, and before 1939 reliance was usually placed on questionnaires or rating scales to elicit a consistent consensus of opinion among those in daily contact with the candidate as superiors, equals or subordinates. During the war, however, the selection of recruits for the Army has included personal interview by the Personnel Selection

E

Officer. The selection of officers included "facing situations" under observation and discussion by members of a Board consisting of a presiding colonel, a military testing officer, a psychiatrist (a doctor qualified in psychology and the treatment of nervous and mental patients) and a psychologist. These War Office Selection Boards (W.O.S.B.s) might well be adapted for staffing industry with managers and foremen—experienced business men taking the place of military members. The personal interview will undoubtedly be developed for assessing the temperament of the ordinary industrial recruit. It requires a trained interviewer who will not, for instance, moralize, or put leading questions, or speak in "a certain tone of voice" and who, though keeping conversation informal, will yet be covering a set of questions uniform for all interviewed.

In conclusion it may be asked, what happens to those eventually rejected by these tests of various types? Does testing mean the detection of a permanently unemployable sediment? The answer already suggested is that most of those rejected for some jobs will be suitable for other jobs. Liability to boredom, for instance, is one of the main obstacles to efficiency in repetition work and mass production, and those who get bored are the more intelligent, extraverted and creatively minded. It follows that workers rejected by tests for responsible jobs are precisely the "elect" for the repetition work. Yet undoubtedly some cases unsuitable for any efficient industrial work may be discovered. Their work may not be worth their normal time wage and the cost of supervision and other overheads in any available job. The choice then lies between subnormal terms of employment, or unemployment, at least while the worker is being medically treated.

§3 ACTUAL SELECTION PRACTICE AND ITS CONSEQUENCES

Much criticism has been levelled against the selection procedure just outlined, but it must be judged by its results as compared to the results of its neglect in the majority of firms. In the typical factory, mine, building firm or service industry, the output and the absence, accident and turnover rates of workers on the same job vary widely, and vary in a way that shows up inefficiency in the choice of workers. The range of the variation of output even in jobs and factory environment that seem quite uniform is surprising. The percentage variation from the average output of the least and the most productive workers in eight groups (spinning, weaving and winding cotton, and making cigarettes by hand) was found to range from "lows" of 65 to 92 per cent up to "highs" of 107 to 132 per cent. Inspection work showed a still wider variation between individuals in speed and accuracy.[1] The form of the variation of outputs of individuals within each group is as significant as their wide range. It will be noted that the "lows" are as far from 100 denoting the average individual output in the groups, as the "highs." Extremes are, in short, symmetrically disposed about the average; and this is in consonance with the "normal" distribution of innate physical and mental qualities discussed in Chapter I; but it is not in consonance with an effective selection. The least productive workers at the tail end should have been eliminated, leaving the distribution of outputs lopsided, the plus extremes more frequent than the minus.

Accidents, absence and labour turnover are, on the other hand, too lopsided in their distribution. Individuals are left in work, often dangerous to themselves (and their mates) who can be shown to be persistently accident prone. For instance, London bus drivers having more than five accidents in their first year of driving had an average of 2.86, 2.57, 2.21, and 2.79 in the four subsequent years, while drivers having no accidents in their first year had an average in the subsequent four years of only 1.11, 1.18, 1.36 and 1.09 accidents. Proneness of individuals to sickness absence similar to that for accidents also occurs in industry. In a sample of 4,500 women in five armament factories, one-eighth of the individuals were responsible for about two-thirds of the total time lost through sickness.[2] Labour turnover normally also concentrates on a relatively small proportion of the factory personnel, but the "rolling stones" are often the new-comers or the very young (as instanced in the next chapter) and it is difficult to disentangle innate proneness to leave one factory for another from mere failure to settle down.

[1] Industrial Health Research Board, Reports 17, 20, 23, 63.
[2] Industrial Health Research Board, Reports 84, 86.

The reasons are fairly obvious for this concentrated incidence of inefficiency—the persistent employment of workers of low productivity and of high accident and absence rates. The average young person, and the adult, too, does not properly seek out the jobs that would match his capacities; and the average employer does not seek out the particular individuals who would match the vacancies he has. Children still at school, like the boy who wanted to become a customs officer because he "would see a variety of places and travel"[1] have rather ill-informed or else trivial "side issue" ideas on what is involved in the jobs they fancy. The range of jobs they think of is necessarily limited by their environment, and what they fancy is not necessarily what they will prove fit for. In any case, fancy it or not, or fit for it or not, young people (and older persons too) can only have a chance to find employment at what is available; they will take a job because it is easy to get. This is particularly true in small communities or in districts that specialize in localized industries where the range of choice is narrow.

Often enough the job is made available by the influence of relations or friends of the family with little reference to the young person's capacity or desires, and where the family income is barely sufficient, a boy or girl may have to take the most paying job available. Since most skilled jobs require apprenticeship with a lower remuneration while learning, the economic attraction is toward unskilled jobs, however suitable for a skilled craft the child may be. The average applicant thus cannot, or does not, take thought in applying for a job, and the average employer is usually just as thoughtless. In a small firm he may rely on giving the once-over personally and be content if the worker looks neat and proves obedient, respectful and docile; in larger firms, selection is delegated either to the foreman or to a special personnel or labour officer, who may in the case of youngsters give some weight to the opinion of schoolmasters or the local juvenile employment service and, in the case of adults, look at their previous experience. Often superficial appearance and manner is decisive, both largely

[1]Valentine and Ritchie, *Journal of National Institute of Industrial Psychology*, October 1928.

measures of home environment rather than of the innate possibilities of the candidate.

As against the wide variability of output and the proneness of certain workers to accident, absenteeism and labour turnover associated with casual methods of getting and giving jobs, what have more scientific selection methods achieved? Attention has already been drawn to the higher proportion of young persons from Birmingham schools who stayed four years in a job when they were vocationally guided by the use of psychological tests. From the employers' standpoint this means reduction of labour turnover costs. Accident rates, too, can be reduced by the spotting of accident prone persons through specially devised tests, and then taking care not to employ them in dangerous processes such as explosive filling. A correlation has already been established by psychologists between the results of certain tests applied to apprentices and their subsequent accident history; boys getting the 25 per cent lowest marks in three tests (largely for quick reaction and co-ordination) had, for instance, twice as many accidents on the average as the higher marked boys.[1] Workers particularly prone to absence due to more or less chronic sickness can also be spotted by physical examination and treated medically before their return to industry, perhaps in some more healthy department. Finally, the workers likely to have a particularly low output in specific jobs can be discovered beforehand and might be assigned to jobs more suited to them.

When by careful placement in accordance with tests, repetition jobs are given to those who do not suffer from monotony, promotion accorded to those who are found by temperament and intellect suitable for shouldering responsibility, worrying jobs such as some inspection processes to those who test as imperturbable; then the quantity and quality of output per man will rise, and the human cost of producing any given output will fall.

§4 TRAINING

After, if not before, selection, most workers in modern industry have to be trained. Training may be distinguished

[1] Industrial Health Research Board, Reports 55, 68.

from education as preparation for a specific job, rather than for life and work in general. The essential question is therefore for what sort of job the training is designed. Jobs in industry are familiarly distinguished as skilled, semi-skilled or unskilled, but it is not always realized that a skilled job means one that is not specialized, but requires all-round knowledge and ability. It is usually the semi-skilled job which is highly specialized, and an unskilled job usually involves heavy labour. Looking back at Table 8, page 66, skilled work would include the "crafts," unskilled work, "body work," and semi-skilled work, the hand work and much of the machine work. Training is usually considered unnecessary for heavy labour; semi-skilled work needs anything from a day to one or two months; skilled work is conventionally taken to need up to six years. But while semi-skilled work being specialized may need training for each new job, all-round skill, usually learned by apprenticeship early in life, does not require training every time a worker changes employers.

Henry Ford maintained that in his motor works[1] in 1920 the length of time required to become proficient in the various occupations was about as follows; 43 per cent of all jobs required not over one day's training; 36 per cent required from one day to one week; 6 per cent required from one to two weeks; 14 per cent required from one month to one year; 1 per cent required from one to six years—these jobs required great skill, as in tool-making and die-sinking.

Perhaps Mr. Ford did not count the training of skilled men that he did not undertake in his own works, but certainly outside mass-production factories the proportion of skilled workers requiring years or, at least, months of training for their job is much greater. Ford's statement, however, conveys the wide range in the training time required for modern industry. In consequence, a wide variety of training practices is adopted, including apprenticeship, learnership, up-grading and technical schooling.

By apprenticeship, the traditional training of the individual craftsman, the young apprentice is bound at a wage lower than normal to an employer or master, who contracts in

[1] *My Life and Work* (1924), p. 110.

return to teach him all the particulars of a trade. This procedure is still adopted where an all-round unspecialized "mastery" of a trade is required—often in conjunction with technical schooling to give scientific background. The engineering, building, furniture, shipbuilding and printing industries use apprenticeship because of the wide variety of jobs these industries offer and the adaptability required of certain workers. But as factories, departments of factories, and single machines tend to get specialized even in these trades, employers, while benefiting from an apprentice's low rate of pay, may fail to provide all-round training. For this reason among others, apprenticeship is losing in importance.

Where jobs are less variegated, and less adaptability is required, up-grading the unskilled into jobs more and more skilled is often resorted to. On the railways an engine cleaner may be up-graded into a fireman, and then as he gains experience, into a driver of engines of greater and greater importance; and similar up-grading schemes are found in iron and steel, coal mining and agriculture. Learnership as practised in the textile, clothing and distributive industries is a modification of apprenticeship, and merges in turn into mere "picking-up" by experience and by occasional help from mates—a matter of learning by trial and error.

The training procedures hitherto described assume that the existing traditional methods of work are efficient and all that the new-comer has to do is to be instructed by the old hands or merely watch them and thus pick their methods up. But motion study described in Chapter V has shown that a job may often be more efficiently and easily carried out if it is analysed and reconstructed afresh. Such "redeployment" can only be carried out in the factory if workers, preferably new workers, are deliberately instructed in the new methods. Hence the advantages of a training school staffed by teachers imbued with the new methods, either at a technical school or college, or in the factory itself. Unfortunately workers are, in England, seldom given time off during working hours, and have to attend technical schools and colleges at night, when, to quote an official report, instruction is "unattractive to many young persons who have done a full day's work, and, though the small minority who do attend doubtless derive great benefit, they are hardly in a condition to obtain full value from the instruction."[1] The Education Act of 1944 is introducing full-time technical schools for children between eleven and fifteen, and later sixteen, and part-time day continuation schools between leaving full-time school and eighteen. Presumably the technical night school for youngsters will gradually be eliminated.

Training schools in the factory itself, often known as vestibule schools, can teach (as was proved in two wars) specific jobs and operations of narrow range with high efficiency. Instructors can be appointed who have ability to teach, incentives and output targets applied, and quality and economy of work specially watched on exactly the same machines as are to be used in actual production.

In contrast, the usual practice of learning or "picking up" by experience is a costly and inefficient process. Rates of accidents are often exceptionally high in the early days of work on a new job. The daily output on many jobs not repetitive increases only slowly in quantity and quality and economy; the learning "curve" takes a long time (and often only progresses in stages, the curve showing a series of steps) before reaching a maximum. Labour turnover, too, is higher among workers new to a factory, suggesting a parallel with the high infant mortality of those new to the world in general. In one American factory where a detailed analysis was made, the labour turnover among workers in their first three months was found to be ten times as fast as among workers who had been there a year.[2]

This high turnover among new-comers may be due as much to unfamiliarity with their social environment as unfamiliarity with the job, and points to the need of careful "induction." By induction or settling in is meant introducing the individual new worker to his supervisor and mates, warning him of danger points in his work, informing him, often by an "employees' manual," of his terms of employment, the rules of discipline, and welfare facilities; and gradually, as his interest deepens, answering his questions

[1]Committee on Industry and Trade, Final Report, 1929, p. 208.
[2]U.S. Public Health Bulletin 106, pp. 166-9.

about the purpose of his job and the place of "his" factory and firm in the industrial system as a whole, and about the whole set-up of manager-worker relations. A worker is not fully trained for his job in an organization, unless he understands that organization and his part in it.

Training in and for the factory is likely to be highly specialized and to prepare a worker only for one job or a limited range of jobs. Training outside the factory, on the other hand, can be undertaken to train a worker for several jobs, or at least for a job other than he is engaged in and thus make him more mobile. This, as will be argued later, should reduce unemployment due to over-supply of workers in a particular industry.

CHAPTER X

TYPES OF WORKER: AGE AND SEX

§1 The YOUNG AND OLD WORKER

THE last chapter was concerned with the selection and training of individual workers. But an employer is often faced with a more fundamental question: shall he change the entire type of worker from which to select individuals? The problem was familiar in both world wars when military call-up of men required dilution and the substitution of women for men in the factories. A similar problem arises when the raising of the school-leaving age and lower birth rates cut down the supply of young people, and when these lower birth rates together with lower death rates leave a higher proportion of old persons in the population.

Man-power shortages and these current changes in the sources of man-power make it important to discuss the comparative availability and efficiency of men and women, and of various age groups. In agreements for hours of work and rates of wages separate provisions are normally made for women and for yearly age-groups below twenty-one, as a whole category or type, if not for the old. Types of workers are thus recognized for the practical purposes of industry regardless of the merits of the individual within the category. We shall begin with the young and the old age groups and proceed in later sections to the relative efficiency and availability of women, and their wage rates.

Census reports and statistics of the numbers nationally insured distinguish the younger age groups, so that it is possible to estimate the man-power lost to various industries by raising the school-leaving age. According to the last British census (1931), 3.8 per cent of all occupied persons were fourteen or fifteen years of age. But if we take the insured wage and salary earners only, these young persons formed, in the normal pre-war year 1936, 6.6 per cent of the total insured. Large industries (employing over 80,000 of all ages) which occupied the highest percentage of fourteen- and fifteen-year-old insured persons were: cardboard boxes and stationery 15.2 per cent; cocoa and sugar confectionery 14.9 per cent; laundries 13.0 per cent; distributive trades 10.7 per cent; and printing 10.6 per cent. These will be the large industries most hit in man-power with the raising of the school-leaving age. When this age becomes sixteen, the whole of the percentages of the total working force just given will indeed no longer be available.

Further reduction of juvenile man-power will occur by reason of the fall in the birth rate. During the period since 1936 fewer children have reached the age of fourteen as a result of a lower number of births fourteen years previously, i.e., from 1922 onwards; a fall only partly counterbalanced by the reduced infant and juvenile death rates. Between 1922 and 1940 birth rates fell heavily as Table 19 shows, so that in Britain during the two years 1945-6 the new entrants into insurable employment aged fourteen and fifteen were only 482,000 as against 560,000 in the two years 1937-8.

Despite the loss in man-power involved, aggravating the fall in the proportion of young persons in the population, there are strong arguments for persisting in the policy of raising the school-leaving age. It is a policy that will increase the efficiency of the future working population positively and negatively. Positively, extended education will increase physical and mental adaptability; negatively, it will prevent children going into dull and repetitive occupations and having their minds and bodies cramped and stunted, at an age when mind and body are growing and particularly impressionable. In many industries the majority of jobs young people obtain are blind-alley, that is they do not even train the children to some particular task which they can continue in later life. In distribution, for instance, errand boys are used till they are sixteen, but after that many of them have to find work in other industries.

It is generally agreed that Britain must rely in future on human rather than material resources. The avoidance of such dead ends and the general conservation and development of the latent powers of the young in all sections of the community will lead to greater prosperity in the long run, than satisfying the immediate needs of man-power. In any case, the employment of young persons is at a low rate of earning (see table on page 144) and is, by many tests, inefficient at least when the customary long hours are imposed on them. In Britain the law still allows young persons sixteen to eighteen to work a full forty-eight hours weekly with occasional overtime. Juvenile accident and labour turnover rates are particularly high, largely due, respectively, to immaturity (including the propensity of boys to "lark") and to the over-hasty acceptance of jobs. These hazards peculiar to youth and their economic and social costs have already been pointed out (Chapters III and IX); at sixteen, children educated up to that age may be expected to have more judgment and more knowledge by which to judge than at fourteen.

As the proportion of people at younger ages falls, that at older ages, such as over sixty, will rise owing to the higher birth rates sixty years or so ago, and to the fall in death rates to-day. More and more people will, in the immediate future, arrive at the usual retiring ages of sixty and sixty-five, more and more will be kept alive after that age, and the question arises whether or not these old people should be encouraged or discouraged to retire. In the days of high unemployed rates, retirement used to be urged; but with man-power shortage the feasibility must be explored of employing aged persons more extensively. At the last British census (1931) 838,000 persons out of a total of 3,316,000 over sixty-five were gainfully occupied—a quarter of all old people over sixty-five, and 4.0 per cent of occupied persons of all ages. By 1951 the total over sixty-five, forecast by the Registrar-General[1] is 5,511,000, a quarter of which would yield 1,377,700 as the number likely to be occupied. With improved health conditions and medical service the fraction of old people fit to work should, however, have increased. Possibly while the proportion of total occupied man-power formed by the young workers aged fourteen to sixteen falls from 3.8 to 0 per cent, the proportion formed by the old workers over sixty-five will have risen from 4.0 per cent to, say, 7.0 per cent, almost making up the deficiency.

Naturally, absenteeism from short-term sickness and,

[1] *Current Trend of Population in Great Britain.* Cmd. 6358, 1942.

perhaps accidents, will be higher for the old than the young. The rise with age in short-term sickness rates (up to 26 weeks) is evident in Table 16. At fifty-five to fifty-nine a man's sickness absence is about double what it is at twenty to twenty-nine. Turnover from death and long-term disablement will also be higher;[1] but from other reasons, such as seeking another job, probably lower. Old people's output must also be expected

TABLE 16: CALENDAR DAYS LOST FROM SHORT-TERM SICKNESS PER YEAR BY AGE AND SEX, SAMPLE OF ALL INDUSTRIES, 1921-3[2]

(1) Age Last Birthday	MEN		SINGLE WOMEN[3]		MARRIED WOMEN	
	(2) Thousands Insured	(3) DAYS LOST (Sample)	(4) Thousands Insured	(5) DAYS LOST (Sample)	(6) Thousands Insured	(7) DAYS LOST (Sample)
16-19	1,303	4.41	1,103	5·53	8	26.88
20-24	1,588	4·69	1,100	6·09	102	16·45
25-29	1,250	4.69	548	5·95	153	12·18
30-34	1,122	4·97	310	6·09	145	10·71
35-39	1,047	5·25	220	6·37	134	10·78
40-44	973	5·60	171	7·07	121	11·06
45-49	901	6·30	143	7·98	99	11·69
50-54	763	7·70	116	9·03	72	12·81
55-59	603	9·73	94	10·36	47	14·07
60-64	446	12·95	69	12·81	29	17·08

to average lower than normal. Yet though comparatively inefficient, many old people would probably be personally more contented employed, at least part-time, than wholly unemployed. On balance, it seems important in national and human interests to make adjustments in organization so as to employ

[1]For incidence of short and long-term cases, see R. Padley, "Studies in Age and Wastage in Industrial Populations," *British Journal of Social Medicine*, October 1947.

[2]Source: Sir A. W. Watson, "National Health Insurance: A Statistical Review." *Statistical Journal*, 1927, Part III.

[3]And Widows.

old people—adjustments such as part-time working and lower minimum times rates of wages for specific older age-groups, similar to the lower rates at the other end of the scale for the very young.

Before proceeding to problems of women's employment, the fact should be noted that men and women whether in or out of industry have a different age-structure. In western civilization women survive longer than men but, owing to marriage, leave industry earlier. Two key comparisons sum up the situation. At the last British census (1931) 6.6 per cent of all men, but 8.1 per cent of all women were sixty-five or over; 25.2 per cent of all occupied men, but 47.0 per cent of all occupied women, were under twenty-five. An important source for increasing man-power in industry is thus the middle-aged and older women, when their children are no longer dependent.

§2 WOMEN'S EMPLOYMENT: COMPARATIVE WAGE RATES

The possibilities of women for supplying the increased man-power so sorely needed arouses acute controversy. The main economic issue is the relation of women's wages to their efficiency, an issue enshrined in the phrase "equal pay for equal work." The whole question teems, indeed, with phrases such as "doing a family man out of a job," "woman's sphere is the home," many of them indicating ignorance and irrational emotion. Not all men are married, and only about half the men employed have children dependent on them, now partly supported by family allowances. Moreover, women's employment, in reality, often helps men's employment. Many industries such as textiles and clothing could hardly be carried on at all without employing women as well as men. The two are in "joint demand" and a man would be "done out of his job" if women were *not* employed.

Though the economist must clear his own mind of emotional phraseology and get to know real industrial conditions, he must understand that the behaviour he is observing, even that of the real business (as against purely "economic") man, is partly conditioned by these emotions. Many employers are swayed by moral rather than economic considerations such that certain work is "unsuitable" for women or that married women ought not to be employed at all. The phrase "woman's sphere is the home," popular in business circles, even suggests that no woman, married or single, should be employed in industry at all, and to some the "problem" of woman's employment implies that every woman in industry is a "problem." Two wars which could not have been won without women munition workers, and an acute post-war man-power shortage have been needed to convince the business community that the additional supply of labour provided by women is a national asset, not a liability.

There are real enough social and health problems involved in women's employment, apart from economic considerations, but these are not so much inherent as connected with double-duty employment, when women with family responsibilities also take on industrial work. In selecting individuals, it has already been pointed out, employers may be taking on a load of "home" difficulties. This applies particularly to women on night work who try to run a home by day. In the nursing profession, where such double duty is excluded, night work is not found inherently harmful to women. The Royal Commission on Equal Pay took the evidence of eight medical experts. It is remarkable with what unanimity their several memoranda fail to find any inherent "physiological or psychological reasons . . . which render women (i) unsuited to particular operations, (ii) less efficient than men in occupations for which they are in general none the less suited." Some reasons, not inherent, were, however, pointed out, such as "double duty" and the industrial apparatus at present either not designed for human capacities at all, or exclusively for men's capacities.

Clearing popular but apparently false notions about the relative physical and psychological capacity of women out of the way, the economist may first observe the facts as to the relative wage rates of men and women and then try to estimate how far the differences are justified by (§3, below) the efficiency and demand and (§4) the supply conditions of women's labour. This interpretation follows the lines of the "apparatus of thought" built up by economics. But though the foreground of the economic argument is clear of emotional factors, plenty of non-economic emotional and social conditions and conventions will be discovered lurking in the background which influence both the demand for and the supply of women. The purely economic approach is a useful opening gambit, but it must not exclude these other conditions in the final analysis.

The outstanding fact of the immediate foreground is that in the wages structure described in Chapter VII and illustrated in Table 13, women's wage rates come very low. It is not possible to show comparable statistics throughout industry in one comprehensive table. But the following comparisons to be found in officially published documents are indicative of the relationship holding between men's and women's wage rates.

(i) For some fifty industries, minimum wage rates for the lowest rated grades of men and of women (usually engaged in similar unskilled or semi-skilled work) are fixed and published by the Trade Boards (now called Wages Councils) described in Chapter XIII. In 1936 the average of all these minimum rates were for men just over 1s. per hour, for women just under 7d. per hour or about 58 per cent of the men's rate. Since then, the gap has closed slightly. In 1946 the average of men's hourly rates was just over 1s. 7d., of women's just over 1s.,—a ratio of 63 per cent.

(ii) The average *earnings* per hour for all grades, skilled and unskilled, are occasionally investigated by the Ministry of Labour for a wide variety of manufactures. The following table separates the average for adult men and women and for youths and girls.

AVERAGE HOURLY EARNINGS

			Men	Women	Youths	Girls
1938, Oct.	..	..	17.7d.	8.9d.	6.8d.	5.0d.
1944, July	..	..	29.1d.	17.3d.	12.2d.	9.50d.

It appears that in 1938 the adult women's hourly earnings were 51 per cent of the men's. By 1944 they were still below 60 per cent.

(iii) Standard or basic time rates agreed upon by voluntary collective bargaining between employers' associations and trade unions or in Joint Industrial Councils are published from time to time by the Ministry of Labour. In August 1946, these rates indicated proportions of 55 to 70 per cent of men's pay (according to industry) for women's pay, with about the same average of 63 per cent, as did the Trade Board rates. Piece rates follow the same pattern since, as explained in Chapter VIII, they are usually fixed to yield earnings at a predetermined percentage above these basic time rates.

(iv) Some Wages Councils publish the whole structure of rates and not just minimum rates for the lowest paid grades. Table 13 (page 102), used as a fairly typical example of such a wage structure, shows that in the same grades, such as cooks, women got from 67 to 73 per cent of the men's wage—slightly higher than typical of the proportion of women to men's basic wages. But it will be seen that unskilled men received a higher wage than all grades of women, except head cooks and supervisors.

§3 EFFICIENCY AND DEMAND CONDITIONS OF WOMEN'S LABOUR

The interpretation of the much lower wage rates of women which first suggests itself is that owing to their inferior efficiency the demand for their labour is lower. Efficiency may be tested, as practised throughout this book, by objective measures like output, labour turnover and absence.

The output of men and women is difficult (and accident rates almost impossible) to compare, since the two sexes are seldom employed on the same job in the same factory. Women are treated as a "type," and similarly jobs are treated as "of the type" of women's work or of men's work. This segregation works unfairly on individual women who deviate upwards from the types either in being capable of men's work or capable of a particularly high output on women's work, paid on time rate. The segregation also precludes the setting of a rate for the job regardless whether men or women receive it, from measuring automatically, in piece earnings, equal pay for equal work. Where unbiased, unemotional opinion can be obtained, an employer will usually state that on work where women are already employed, they are more efficient in quantity ·and quality of work than the men who might be substituted for them. This is particularly so in operations requiring dexterity and the endurance of monotony—a large field of modern manufacturing which includes operating and tending of machines, filling and assembly work, and inspection.

British and American experience of comparative labour turnover of the sexes, apart from raw recruits to industry, is that in times of industrial depression men have a lower rate than women but not always in times of boom and full employment.[1] Women's turnover is fairly constant during depression and boom, and is attributable chiefly to women giving up industrial work for home duties (mainly owing to marriage); but men's turnover varies greatly. The chief reason for its height during booms, is men's greater desire for higher wages.

When undeterred by fear of unemployment men often leave one factory for another, on the chance of an offer of higher pay. If full employment or at least a high employment is to be assured in future, lower pay to women will probably not be justifiable by citing much higher costs due to labour turnover. With eight years between normal entry into industry and the average age at marriage (see Chapter III), women's annual turnover rates due to marriage will probably be considerably less than the men's rate due to attempts to better their position. The costly exception occurs in occupations where a long specialized training period is needed. Here retirement on marriage soon after the training has finished, fails to give an economic return for the cost of training.

Comparative absence rates of men and women are cited in Chapter III and show that married women have on the average a much higher, and single women a slightly higher, rate than men in industries where both sexes are employed. The difference between married and single women is greater than between men and single women. These differences are partly due to differences in sickness rates, partly to other causes. Table 16 based upon the fullest English official inquiry into National Health Insurance experience (covering 500,000 men and 400,000 women) shows the calendar (not merely working) days lost per year by cases of sickness lasting four

[1] See e.g. Florence, *Economics of Fatigue and Unrest*, pp. 175-7.

days to twenty-six weeks, including the first three days of those cases. The experience of men, of single and widowed women, and of married women is given separately at different ages. Up to the age of forty-nine, single women have about a quarter more days of sickness than men, but after fifty the gap closes in. Single women do not claim sickness any more often than men, but they stay sick longer. Possibly many of them have not the same financial need as men to return to work before being fully cured.

Married women both claim more often and stay sick longer—even longer than single women. Young married women, twenty to twenty-four, have particularly high sickness rates, almost twelve calendar days per year more than the men, and over ten days per year more than the single women of the same ages; but it can be seen from Table 11 that most women in industry are single, and are younger in age than men and that single women, sixteen to twenty-nine (forming the bulk of employed women) have a lower average sickness rate than men over forty-five.

The difference in absence generally between married and single women, wider than that between single women and men, illustrates the importance of separating the factor of double-duty from that of women's employment at large. The difference is attributable partly to the high sickness rates among young married women, presumably due to pregnancy, but also (especially at older ages) to absence not due to the absentee's own sickness.

Under present conventions if anything goes amiss with any member of the family, it is a woman (usually the wife and mother) who has to stay at home—away from the factory—to attend to the emergency. Possibly if the older married women without dependants were tabulated with the single, while married and single women with family responsibilities were not included, the women's absence rates would be much the same as men's.

A solution, practical for women with home duties, and feasible in many factories has been suggested in Chapter IV in the form of half-time shifts. Women without home duties would work full-time, women with home duties, half time at factory, half-time at home. In both cases the average of absenteeism from the factory would probably be reduced.

The much higher absence rate of married women, and the slightly higher rate of single women certainly seems a good reason for a somewhat lower demand for women. Absence, Chapter III pointed out, means a higher overhead cost on each unit of output, since a lower output from the whole factory must carry the same fixed expenses for foremen, management, heat, light and depreciation on machines. There is therefore a risk in employing women as a class or "type" that overhead or indirect charges will be higher per unit of output, and to compensate themselves employers are justified in paying a little less in the direct costs, i.e., wages per piece, but only a little less, particularly if, as suggested earlier, the full-time women were all free of home duties. The great differences in women's piece wages, 35-50 per cent short of the men's, cannot be accounted for merely by the recorded differences in absenteeism.

Women's wage rates, then, appear too low compared to men's, in the light of the demand for women to be expected from their only slightly lower efficiency. Their comparative wages appear to be no true index of the comparative value of their work to the employer or of their contribution to national wealth.

If it be true that employers get a better bargain for their money from women, are not more women likely to be employed? Yet, apart from the compulsory direction of war years, there has been little increase in the proportion of women employed compared to men. Women are not increasingly selected for employment. British censuses for the last seventy or eighty years have shown occupied women remaining about 30 per cent of the total occupied. One explanation offered for this paradox is that though women are as efficient as men, or almost so, in many industries, and their wages low in relation to their comparative efficiency, these industries are limited in range. The limited field of demand for women's labour is held to explain the stability of the proportion of women employed, and also their lower wage, since a large supply of women is competing for a small field of demand. Before analysing the supply side let us examine the exact limits of the field of women's employment.

Industries classified by the Ministry of Labour for insurance against unemployment may be divided into industries employing almost exclusively men, employing men and women fairly equally, and employing predominantly women.

Just before the war, large industries employing men almost exclusively were agriculture, fishing, mining, building, public utility, transport, and some branches of manufacture such as brick-making, iron and steel, marine and constructional engineering, ship-building, and the earlier processes in woodworking. The number employed here was roughly 4,500,000. On the other hand large industries employing women predominantly, were catering and laundries, clothing and textile industries and (outside the insurance scheme) personal service—with a total in employment perhaps of 3,750,000; and large industries employing men and women on proportions not very unequal, were the distributive trades, commerce, professional, and Government service, and branches of manufacture such as food, drink and tobacco, and paper and printing—with a total in employment of 4,250,000. In short, the field for the employment of women is not so restricted as commonly supposed. To judge from the industries quoted (employing about four-fifths of all workers) the employment in predominantly women's industries and mixed industries is not far from double the employment in industries almost exclusively men's. And on the whole the field of women's employment should be extending, since the demand for labour is increasing relatively in the service industries and in the later (and usually lighter) processes such as mass assembly, where women can be most efficiently employed.

The labour-saving machines continually being introduced by the industrial revolution save men's muscle, but often introduce a demand for the dexterity and endurance of monotony possessed by women. The wage structure, as was said in Chapters VII and VIII, is largely based on tradition. But tradition harking back to the phase of industry when muscle and skilled craftsmanship were most in demand, may well be out of date in its evaluation of men's as against women's work.

§4 SUPPLY CONDITIONS OF WOMEN'S LABOUR

The possible field for women's employment in industry, though wider than often supposed, and probably expanding, is certainly less than that for men's employment; but to explain the actual "woman power" employed and their comparative wage rates, the extent of demand must be related to the extent of the supply. Some economists seem to assume that because roughly as many women are born as men (and more survive to old age), therefore the number of women available for industry is as great, if not greater, than the number of men. There are, in fact, certain social conventions and home commitments limiting the available supply of women. With certain exceptions (where the family is very poor and extra earnings are urgent, or where women have learned a skilled trade, or where industry is carried on at home by out-workers) working women customarily leave industry on marriage. No rise in wages easily contemplated by employers will alter their behaviour in this respect wherever this custom is honoured, and under such conventions married women (more than half the number of all women) are, for all practical purposes of the labour market, non-existent. The necessity of keeping up a home for children will normally have priority over industrial employment, and except in times of emergency society conventionally deems any married woman to have such a home. The census of 1921 showed that only 9.1 per cent of married women were gainfully occupied in industry, though 69 per cent of all spinsters were so occupied.

A further social convention is that people, and particularly women should live in families. A daughter will find it made difficult for her to seek employment in an area other than where her father works—partly for the very reason of her lower wage. She is in "joint supply" with her family, almost unable to move without them. Areas where employers demanded more women were thus, before the war, unable to draw fully from areas like South Wales or the North-East Coast, where industries were mainly of the type employing few women, and plenty of unoccupied women were available.

Though felt in the First World War, these limitations in the supply of women's labour were brought out still more forcibly in the last war. In spite of compulsory direction (or threat of it) and of the undoubted call of patriotism, over half the total of adult women, aged fourteen to fifty-nine, remained mainly housewives. Clearly, if this half of all women were not available for industry or the Services in the crisis of 1941-44, they will not be available for industry in normal peace time.

So far from the field of demand being more limited than the supply of women relatively to men, the opposite is more likely to be true. The apparent stability in the proportion of women employed is due not to the limit imposed by their efficiency upon the demand for them, but rather to the limits conventionally imposed upon their supply.

Why, if women workers are scarce relatively to men, do not their wage rates rise? The answer probably lies in their inferior bargaining power relative to the men workers as well as relative to the employer. Women have less bargaining strength because they are less united and "solid" in the terms they will insist upon.

"Fathers of families expect a family wage, and since most workmen either are, have been, or expect to be fathers of families, an effective majority of all male trade unionists will insist on a family wage being written in their "collective" bargain with the employers. They meet the employers in a solid front with an agreed common rule for which all are prepared to strike if necessary. Not so among women. Among working women there is not one standard upon which a sufficient majority can agree and force upon the minority. For there are probably as many girls industrially employed who are living with their parents, and not wanting full keep, as girls and women living alone or trying to keep themselves and support dependants to boot. There can be no agreement to strike for wages sufficient to meet the demands upon the women supporting others, and any wage adequate to their needs that may be secured is likely to be undercut by the low standard of requirements of girls partially supported by others."[1]

Women workers' "solidarity" is thus inferior to men's, yet both have to bargain with an increasingly "solid" association of employers. If women were as staunch to trade union organi-

[1] Florence, "A Statistical Contribution to the Theory of Women's Wages," *Economic Journal*, March 1931.

zation as men, they could (if our interpretation is correct) narrow the gap between men's and their wages without causing unemployment among themselves by checking demand. The increased employment of women, so necessary if Britain's labour-power is to be adequate, is not so much a matter of maintaining and stimulating demand as of stimulating the supply for the industry. This can be done by raising wages, while changing, if possible, social conventions and industrial practices and thus enabling more women to offer their services. The provision of mothers' helps and the extension of works' canteens, British Restaurants and war-time nurseries, for instance, would all release women who preferred industrial work to full-time home duties; and the practice of half-time employment would enable women with lesser home duties to do "double half-duties." Industries must also be located where there are spare supplies of married women, or single women tied to their family—a point to be taken up in Chapter XII. If these arrangements seem revolutionary of social life the alternative must be borne in mind: an insufficiently low proportion of industrial workers to total population to maintain Britain's past standard of living in the face of her post-war international position.

PART III

UNEMPLOYMENT

CHAPTER XI

THE INCIDENCE OF UNEMPLOYMENT

§1 PERSONAL INCIDENCE

UNEMPLOYMENT has been defined as the idleness of persons able and willing to work. In Chapter I it was approached as a wastage of national man-power, in Chapter II as a personal, human catastrophe, and in Chapter III as a measurable, costly failure to make efficient use of the human factor. In this chapter the distribution of unemployment will be analysed in more detail, beginning where these chapters left off, at the personal incidence.

When the general level of unemployment is as high as during the inter-war period, seldom less than 10 per cent, the majority of workers are unemployed for economic causes. Because demands for the products of their industry or their services have fallen, a certain proportion must be "laid off" irrespective of any personal characteristic. But whenever or wherever unemployment is low, say the 3 per cent envisaged by Lord Beveridge as constituting full employment, personal characteristics may be the factor of greatest importance in the actual incidence of unemployment.

A theme running throughout this book has been the differences between individual workers or groups of workers in their capacity or willingness to work. Capacity and willingness have been depicted as shading off into one another and it is a simplification of the economist to speak of persons either able and willing to work, or not able or willing. Human beings, as pointed out in Chapter I, vary qualitatively and quantitatively in their capacity if not their willingness, and when demand

153

falls off for a certain proportion of workers, the less able and the less willing are likely to lose their jobs. In short, analysis of unemployment may show an unemployment "proneness" among certain individuals, and a higher incidence in frequency or in severity among certain types of persons.

Among workers leaving employment we have, when discussing labour turnover, distinguished those having to be replaced (and forming the turnover) from those not having to be replaced. Workers leaving and having to be replaced may either have "quit" of their own accord or may have been "discharged" by the employer for inefficiency or breaches of discipline. If, however, an employer has to terminate a worker's employment merely because there is insufficient economic demand for his services, he will not be replaced—American usage conveniently calls this "laying-off" workers. Since the discharged worker is replaced, the *total* of unemployment will only be affected by "lay-offs," but any particular worker may be unemployed either because he is discharged or laid off, or because he quit without finding another job. Unemployment will therefore fall personally on those discharged because (in the opinion of an employer) of their incapacity or unwillingness to work, who have been unable to find another employer. But unemployment will also overtake those who are merely laid off by an employer for lack of economic demand or those who quit and are unable to find another employer.

Are there any types of worker who in these ways appear to suffer a higher frequency or severity of unemployment? There is evidence of such a higher incidence among the older workers and the less skilled. There is little to prove that older people are less in demand now than hitherto, nor are older men more frequently laid off than younger men; but the older man, once he has lost a job, finds it harder than a younger man to get a new job. "The risk of losing one's job is much the same from sixty to sixty-four as it is from thirty-five to forty-four; the risk of being out of a job is half as much again at the later age than at the earlier age; the risk of becoming chronically unemployed, that is to say of being out for more than a year, is two and a half times as great."[1]

[1]Beveridge, *Full Employment in a Free Society*, pp. 70-71.

There is not only greater severity of unemployment among the old at any one time, but the older workers form a higher proportion of the unemployed when total unemployment is low. Official analysis of the unemployed in May 1935, 1936 and 1937, when the total rate of unemployment was decreasing steadily from 15.5 to 12.8 per cent and 10.9 per cent, showed the age group forty-five to sixty-four to form an increasing percentage from 35.4 to 37.9 per cent and 41.2 per cent among the men unemployed; from 19.3 to 20.9 per cent and 23.3 per cent among the women unemployed.[1] With an aggregate unemployment rate down to the full employment level of 3 to 6 per cent, the percentage of older groups among the unemployed would, presumably, rise still higher.

Age is only one personal characteristic, but it certainly affects the degree of capacity to work and probably willingness to move. Other characteristics associated with unemployment have been insufficiently analysed. There is evidence from the Census of Population for England and Wales in 1931 that the unskilled manual workers are more liable to unemployment than the skilled and semi-skilled—the comparable rates were 30.5 per cent and 14.4 per cent; and there is fragmentary evidence that the unemployed are on the average less intelligent than the employed.[2] Data on the proportion of the unemployed at any place or time that are economically quite unemployable, either in the jobs they are seeking or generally, is still more fragmentary.

Assuming high and stable employment in the future, the personal incidence of unemployment will have to be given much greater attention than heretofore. In the next chapter policies will be put forward for preventing unemployment. The bulk of them are economic, urging the maintenance of public and private demand and outlay for products and services. If there are some workers who are below normal in their capacity (or willingness) to produce and serve, or to move where they can produce and serve, only a very intensive demand requiring products and services at all costs (as during

[1]Ministry of Labour *Gazette*, July 1935, July 1937.
[2]N. W. Morton, *Occupational Abilities*; S. Bevington, *Occupational Misfits*.

a war or the aftermath of war) will sweep these sub-normal into employment. Once war's aftermath is passed, however, these less capable or less willing sub-normal workers may be unemployed. To prevent or cure this personal incidence of unemployment, the physiologist and psychologist will have to be called in rather than economists. Neither incapacity nor unwillingness are necessarily immutable.

§2 THE TIME INCIDENCE OF UNEMPLOYMENT

Unemployment is familiarly classified into casual, seasonal, cyclical and secular unemployment. All of these adjectives refer to shorter and longer periods of time during which unemployment develops as a result of fluctuations and other changes in the volume of trade. Unemployment, however, does not necessarily correspond with trade fluctuation. The same or a greater amount of products and services might be produced with fewer employed workers through the substitution of machines (or managers) for men. This technological substitution has been proceeding at different rates in many industries and places, and will be considered in a separate section following upon discussion of the time, industrial and local incidence of unemployment.

The time incidence of unemployment is simplest in the case of seasonal fluctuations of trade, when there is a regular recurrence of unemployment at times known beforehand, and the whole span is one year. Cyclical unemployment recurs at longer, but not at such regular or predictable, intervals. Casual unemployment depends on day-to-day changes in the volume of trade—the non-arrival of ships in port, the completion of a large building, or a rainy or frosty day, halting outdoor production. It is, in miniature, of the same category as unemployment caused by the accidents of trade, such as the outbreak of war or of peace, or the imposition of tariff barriers.

By secular unemployment is meant unemployment corresponding to some long term or "secular" trend in trade, due mainly to a gradual decline in demand. Products may go out of fashion like horse-carriages, saddlery or gas lighting, or, if they are producers' goods, may be discarded owing to some new process; or the industry of a particular country may be losing to that of another.

In the case of three of the four types of time-incidence, the time of incidence is different for different industries. Industries have different, often opposite, seasonal unemployment. Some industries are casual, most not; and accidental events will hit different industries differently. Industries differ again in their secular trend of employment; some grow, while others decline. But in cyclical unemployment, industries suffer together nationally and even internationally. Though some will suffer unemployment less than others, as described in §3, and some lead in the onset of unemployment while others lag, few industries will enjoy particular prosperity for any length of time, while other industries are cyclically depressed. It is for this reason that the time incidence of the cyclical unemployment has drawn so much attention. The whole community suffers at these times of general depression or slump, and the uncertainty of the precise time when this general suffering will set in, if at all, and how long it will last has led to much speculation in various senses of the word.

Speculation, in the sense of forecasting, must be mainly based empirically on past experience, and a long series of observations of twentieth-, nineteenth- and even eighteenth-century trade, has justified the word "cycle" by showing that the recurrence of unemployment has been at periodic intervals, and that unemployment has diminished and increased during the intervals in a fairly regular rhythmic swing down and up. Complete cycles have in the past run through their phases in seven to eleven years, a period long enough to give plenty of latitude to developments and complications.[1]

The seriousness of cyclical unemployment is that it is more or less general to industry and that it is uncertain in its onset, amplitude and duration. Its development sets up forces which are at first not self-rectifying and equilibrium may be upset for a considerable time by vicious circles of events. To take the circle working through labour; workers are "laid off" in one industry, therefore their income falls, therefore they spend less, therefore demand for the products of other industries falls,

[1]*See* especially McGregor, *Enterprise, Purpose and Profit.*

therefore workers in those industries are laid off, therefore
their income falls, and so on, aggravated usually by a general
fall in business confidence. Rectifying forces have in the past
finally established themselves (otherwise the process would not
be a cycle), but not before serious unemployment and loss of
production has occurred, concentrated particularly in certain
industries.

§3 THE INDUSTRIAL INCIDENCE

The wide differences in the unemployment risk of different
industries is brought out forcibly by Table 17. All the fourteen
productive industries distinguished by the Ministry of Labour
which had more than 125,000 workers insured in 1937 are
included. They consist in coal mining and building and
two groups of manufacturing industries, the first six industries
dealing with metals only. The first column gives the proportion of insured workers who were unemployed in August
1932, the month of peak unemployment for industry as a
whole in the 1930-1934 depression. The percentage of unemployment ranges from 10.4 per cent in printing and 11.0 per
cent in baking trades to 49.3 per cent (one worker out of two!)
in the iron and steel industry and 59.8 per cent (three workers
out of five!) in shipbuilding. These figures for a particular day
in one month of the depression were hardly influenced by
casual, though to some extent by seasonal fluctuations.

On the day in question, 22nd August, 1932, the number of
unemployed returned as normally in casual employment was
only just over 3 per cent of the total unemployed. Of the
industries tabulated, only building is subject to any serious
casual unemployment; the other casual occupations are mostly
in service industries like dock labour. A few industries like
cotton were working short-time, however, to spread employment among their workers.

Industries differ considerably in seasonal variation of
employment and (where there is significant variation) in the
times of peak and trough. Judging from the experience of 1924
to 1932[1], the motor industry in summer normally touches
2 per cent and coal mining, cotton and wool about 5 per cent

[1]C. Saunders, *Seasonal Variations in Employment.*

TABLE 17: UNEMPLOYMENT RISK OF DIFFERENT INDUSTRIES AND REGIONS

Industries	Aug. 1932 Per Cent Rate of Unemployed	Season when 2 per cent or more below general level. (Average of 1924-33)	Depth of Cyclical Trough 1932² (per cent)	Secular Trend 1923-37 Total Employed 1937 as per cent of 1923	Region of Localization, if any	Characteristics of products — Capital (Cap.) Durable (Dur.) Export (Exp.) Novelty (Nov.)	Total of Points (Minus for Novelty)
Coal Mining	41·6	Summer	−18	59·4	S. Wales, N.E.	Cap. Exp.	2
Iron and Steel, Melting Puddling, Rolling	49·3	—	−35	101·6	E. Mid., W. Yorks North, W. Yorks.	Cap. Dur.	2
General Engineering	28·8	—	−22	115·8	S.Wales, S.W.Scot.	Cap. Dur.	2
Motor Vehicles, Cycles, Aircraft	22·1	Summer	−20	196·4	W. Mid.	Cap. Dur. Nov.	1
Shipbuilding	59·8	Autumn	−46	91·6	N.E., S.W.Scot.	Cap. Dur. Exp.	3
Electric Cables, Apparatus, Lamps, etc.	12·2	—	−7	265·4	London	Dur. Nov.	0
Miscellaneous Metals	20·3	—	−17	175·6	W. Mid.	Dur.	1
Cotton	33·5	Summer	−15	83·4	Lancs.		1
Woollen and Worsted	26·8	Summer	−14	84·6	W. Yorks.	Exp.	1
Tailoring	19·1	Winter	−1	113·6	W. Yorks.	Exp.	0
Bread, Biscuits, Cakes	11·0	—	−1	115·6			0
Furniture, Upholstery	21·6	Winter	−9	163·5	London	Dur.	1
Printing, Publishing, Book-Binding	10·4	—	+1	127·6			0
Building and Contracting	27·3	Winter	−22	160·9		Dur.	1
All Industries and Services	23·1	—	−9	124·6			

¹ All with over 125,000 employed in 1937.
² Comparison of numbers employed in 1932 with the average of 1929 and 1935.

below their average level of employment. Shipbuilding falls 3 per cent in the autumn. Building, on the other hand, normally has a 6 per cent, tailoring a 5 per cent and the furniture industry a 2 per cent drop in the average level of employment in winter. The others among the fourteen listed industries show no marked seasonal fluctuation. Large industries not listed which have exceptionally high seasonal variation are hotels and boarding-houses (especially at holiday resorts), and dress-making and millinery, both with winter troughs; and pottery, with troughs both in August and mid-winter. The significant point about the industrial incidence of seasonal unemployment is that, like cyclical unemployment, there are industries with heavy and with little fluctuation, but that, unlike cyclical unemployment (measured in the next column) the heavy fluctu-ation of different industries may be converse. Employment may be at its peak in one industry, when it is in a trough in another. This permits "dovetailing" of converse industries to smooth out unemployment locally under a policy of industrial diversi-fication, if workers are willing and capable of switching over from one industry to the other.

The rate of unemployment for certain industries will also be influenced by the secular trend, measured in a further column. The high percentage unemployed in coal mining and the cotton industry, for instance, was largely the result of the general fall in employment over the period 1923 to 1937.

In the main, however, the order of figures of unemploy-ment for August, 1932, corresponds with that of the index of cyclical fluctuations as obtained in Table 17 by comparing the number employed in 1932 (the year of greatest slump) with the fairly prosperous two years at either side of it, 1929 and 1935. The index measures a percentage "dip," the depth of trough between the waves. It is deepest for shipbuilding and iron and steel, with dips of 46 and 35 per cent, shallowest for the baking trades and tailoring, with 1 per cent dips, while printing has no trough at all.

What differences are there in the characteristics of these different industries which may explain these wide divergences between them in the course of cyclical and secular employment? The first feature to strike the eye in the table is that, with one exception, all six industries in the metal group have deeper cyclical troughs than any of the other manufacturing industries. Now metal goods are durable in use. Many of them also serve as instruments to make other goods and to reproduce themselves; they are, in short, mostly capital goods. For both reasons they need not be produced regularly year by year. They can last over the depression phase of the cycle; and new instruments of production for expansion or even for replacement will, in any case, not be wanted while there are fewer goods to make. Though some of the fourteen industries make a wide variety of goods, the quality of durability in use to various degrees can be marked in the table as applying to eight of them. Five are precisely the five industries with the lowest cyclical troughs and none of the remaining three (making the somewhat less durable electrical apparatus and miscellaneous metals and furniture) have a trough of less than 7 per cent. The quality of making capital goods apply to five, all among the six industries with the deepest troughs.

A further salient feature of the table is the secular fall between 1923 and 1937 in the numbers employed in coal mining, shipbuilding, and the cotton and wool industries. Now all these industries exported a large proportion of their output or, as in shipbuilding, produced goods coping with exports. On the other hand, two industries, motor vehicles and electric apparatus, showed almost a doubling or more in employment between 1923 and 1937. In both cases, more so than others in the list of industries, recent scientific discovery and invention have produced a novel type of product which has created completely new demands.

If the fourteen industries are marked *plus* for the qualities of making capital, durable or exportable goods where employment fluctuates and *minus* for making novelties that expand employment, it will be found that this point system accounts (minus signs cancelling out plus) for the broad differences of the unemployment percentages in August, 1932. The cotton industry has a higher, engineering a lower unemployment than the points predict, but while engineering is seasonally stable, cotton, it must be remembered, suffers a summer slump not allowed for by the points.

F

§4 THE LOCAL INCIDENCE

Some industries are localized in the sense that a much greater proportion of their workers is found in certain localities than the proportion of the population working there in all industries. The proportion of British iron and steel smelting and rolling workers that lived in South Wales was (in 1931) 12.38 per cent, but the proportion of the population working in all industries that lived in South Wales only 3.70 per cent. The iron and steel industry may thus be said to be localized in South Wales since it occupied there over three times the all-industry proportion of workers. To use a technical term, it had a *location quotient* in South Wales of 12.38 ÷ 3.70 = 3.3. Again 20.12 per cent of all coal-miners lived in South Wales, so that there coal mining's *location quotient* was as high as 20.12 ÷ 3.70 = 5.4.[1]

In the column last but one of Table 17 the larger regions are given where each of the fourteen industries are localized, if they are localized at all, using as the test a location quotient at least over 2.0[2]

Now a region may suffer severely from unemployment, if industries with high unemployment risks are localized there. For if a disproportionately large number of its workers are engaged in such industries, there will be fewer workers left in the other, less risky, industries to carry on in employment and to contribute to the family income and to the trade of the locality generally.

Can any regions be found in the table that specialize in unemployment-prone industries? Clearly, three: South Wales, where coal mining and iron and steel are localized, the North East Coast where coal mining and shipbuilding are localized, and South West Scotland (including Clydeside) where coal mining and shipbuilding are localized. And these, in fact, contain the largest of the areas, first distinguished as depressed, then as "special," and now known as "development" areas. Though the geographical divisions and regions are wider than the depressed areas, the picture of inequality in local incidence emerges clearly from the divisional unemployment percentages

[1] *See* P. E. P., *The Location of Industry*, Appendix 1.
[2] *ibid.*

in August, 1932: 12.9 per cent each for London and for the South Eastern Division; 27.9 per cent for Scotland; 30.9 per cent for the North Eastern Division; and 39.1 per cent for Wales. These areas were not depressed because they were poor in natural resources, but for the very opposite reason. They were so rich in having coal and iron ore next the sea-board—a combination rare in the world—that workers increased fast (naturally and by migration) in the days when ships and the products of steel smelting were in demand. When this demand fell off cyclically and by secular trend, a great number of workers were left high and dry, without employment. The very fact that the areas were so richly endowed for the earlier and heavier metal processes had made it unnecessary to start lighter industries. Hence few women were occupied for pay in these areas and, when their husbands and fathers became unemployed, could not help in maintaining the family income.

Similarly, localization of cotton in Lancashire and wool in Yorkshire, threatens further depressed areas as a result of possible secular decline in demand, unless other large industries settle there; and there are smaller areas such as the Potteries in North Staffordshire, or Coventry specializing in motor vehicles, where the localization of one industry subject to unemployment puts all the eggs in one fragile basket.

Increased employment since 1920 in the London and the Midland areas compared to Wales and the North has often been alluded to as the "southward drift of industry." There is no doubt about the geographical differences in the growth of employment, but the picture of industries moving south is misleading. What actually happened was that industries which were localized in the Midlands (such as motor vehicles, aircraft engineering and miscellaneous metals) and in London (such as electrical apparatus and furniture) were those that grew fastest nationally, industries localized in South Wales and the North those that grew nationally most slowly or actually declined.[1] Cotton, wool or shipbuilding have not "moved" south but, generally speaking, southern and midland industries (staying where they are) have given more employment; northern and Welsh industries (staying where they are) less.

[1] *See* West Midland Group, *Conurbation*, Table 24.

§5 TECHNOLOGICAL UNEMPLOYMENT

Unemployment may not correspond with the course of trade and production when it is caused by changes in methods of production. Semi-skilled may replace skilled workers, wage earners be replaced by salaried organizers and, above all, machines and technical processes may replace workers generally. Scientific invention and technical progress are likely to continue, and will continue to displace men by machines in many industries. As an immediate consequence production will often increase, and yet there will be less men employed and greater unemployment.

This so-called technological unemployment should, however, set up self-rectifying forces:—

1. More men are employed in making the new machines and capital goods.

2. Since distribution and administration are hardly subject to mechanization at all, more men are employed to handle machine-made goods, the greater is the amount of goods produced as a result of mechanization.

3. Costs and presumably prices are reduced by mechanization, thus liberating consuming power to buy (a) more of the same goods, or (b) more of other goods and services.

These three "compensating" processes can be traced fairly objectively, particularly in the period 1923 to 1938 in the numbers recorded by the Ministry of Labour as employed in certain industries. Evidence of a fast rate of mechanization comes from the Census of Production in a rise between 1924 and 1930 of horse-power capacity per worker in all production from 2.0 to 2.4.[1] Taking the three processes in detail:

(1) Though machine making (i.e., engineering) and other capital goods industries fluctuate violently during the trade cycle, as shown earlier, the general long term trend is undoubtedly upward. Hoffman[2] has shown that the proportion of the

---

[1]For the difficulties in using horse-power as a measure of mechanization, see Florence, *Investment, Location and Size of Plant*, Chapter V, §§ 2 and 3.

[2]*Stadien und Typen der Weltwirtschaft*, 1931.

occupied population formed by workers in industries largely engaged in capital goods (metals and chemicals) rose in the United Kingdom from 8.1 per cent in 1841 to 23.8 per cent in 1901, a period of wide mechanization. Table 17 shows employment in engineering to have risen in 1937 to 115.8 per cent of 1923; employment in electrical engineering (not included in the table) about doubled, from 57,000 in 1923 to 112,000 in 1937.

(2) Distribution and other services have persistently employed a higher proportion of the occupied population at times and places of technical progress, and have increased faster in man-power than other industries. While in 1937, all industries and services (see Table 17) employed 124.6 per cent of the number in 1923, transport and distribution employed 148.4 per cent.

(3a) The frequent effect of mechanization in eventually employing more workers in the very industries that were being mechanized can be traced by comparing changes in the horse-power capacity of an industry's equipment with changes in workers employed. The period 1924 to 1930 was in Britain one of undoubted technical progress. Each of these two years had a production census. In the intervening years the motor and cycle industry raised horse-power capacity per worker 24 per cent, output per worker 29 per cent. But the total output made (and presumably sold) increased so much faster, i.e., by 49 per cent, that 15 per cent more men were employed. Another example is the silk and artificial silk industry where horse-power per worker rose 43 per cent between 1924 and 1930 and output per worker 63 per cent; but since total output rose by 145 per cent, 50 per cent more workers were employed. Other large industries showing substantial mechanization (horse-power per worker increasing in the six years not less than 14 per cent) combined with substantially increased employment (given in brackets) were as follows, according to the Census of Production: Glass (10 per cent), rubber (10 per cent), tobacco (14 per cent), preserved food (14 per cent), paint (15 per cent), musical instruments (22 per cent), electrical engineering (22 per cent), hardware (24 per cent), ink and gum (25 per cent), gloves (31 per cent), furniture (32 per cent), sugar refining (34 per cent), cardboard box (45 per cent), building (46 per cent), aircraft (82 per cent). The increased output and employment in many of these industries were not, of course, entirely due to reduced cost of production and lower prices acting on an elastic demand but also, as in the case of aircraft, due to the new demands for a novelty. But without lowered cost following in most cases upon mechanization demands would undoubtedly not have expanded so greatly.

(3b) Wherever mechanization lowered cost and price, but output did not expand sufficiently to employ more or as many workers as before, it is likely that the elasticity of demand was low and that consumers' total outlay on the product fell. Assuming no fall in total expenditure of consumers, this would release purchasing power for other goods and services. If these were, as in the case of services, not in their turn becoming mechanized, the number of their workers employed should rise. Between 1923 and 1937 employment in consumers' services, such as entertainment, catering and laundry, increased faster even than distribution and transport, as from 100 respectively to 229.6, 172.2 and 166.1. If not eventually increasing employment in its own industry, labour-saving mechanization and organization will thus compensate the original "lay-off" of workers by generating employment in other industries.

Before the self-rectifying forces have achieved this result, however, there may be a wasteful time-lag. Workers "laid off" may be without new employment for months, the time depending partly on their geographical, occupational and industrial mobility or adaptability, but partly on the degree of unemployment from other causes. If technological unemployment comes on top of a general cyclical depression, workers laid off will not have much chance of re-employment, however mobile.

Mobility from job to job was analysed in Part I and allowed to be as important to labour in the economic system as efficiency at a given job. Like efficiency, mobility can be increased through inducements to willingness as well as conducives to the capacity to move. Both will be taken up when seeking, in the next chapter, how to obtain full employment.

§6 THE HARD CORE OF UNEMPLOYMENT

The incidence of unemployment has been divided into three main types; personal, general, and particular to certain industries whether a predictable risk or (as with technological change) an unpredictable uncertainty. This sub-division is of practical significance because it indicates three different types of solution: treatment of persons; general national policy; and mobility of labour between industries, occupations and places helped by local diversification of industries.

Not all cases of unemployment in all countries is covered by this sub-division. In many East European and Oriental countries there is a continued high birth rate with diminishing death rates and consequent rapid increase in population. This increase, without a *higher* increase in the productivity of the country's natural resources or capital equipment, may well account for rising, or at least a dead weight of stable unemployment among the industrial proletariat, just as it accounts for lowered or stationary standards of living among the peasant proprietors.

In Great Britain between 1921 and 1938 the unemployment percentage for industry as a whole fell below 10 per cent only in one year. There was the normal cyclical rhythm in unemployment fluctuating from 17 per cent in 1921 down to 9.7 per cent in 1927 and up again to 21.9 per cent in 1932 and down again to 10.6 per cent in 1937, but the persistence of high unemployment even at the boom phase of the two cycles was new and was often labelled the "hard core" of unemployment. It was partly due to the fact that relatively declining industries were localized in persistently depressed areas where all trades suffered in consequence. In 1937, for instance, the Welsh county of Glamorgan still had an unemployment rate of 23.7 per cent, though in populous industrial counties, such as Middlesex (without London) and Warwickshire, unemployment in 1937 was as low as 4.8 and 4.4 per cent. Apart from the depressed areas, however, unemployment showed a core in 1921-36 considerably harder than before the First World War; in the boom phase of the trade cycle, instead of 9 or 10 per cent, unemployment before 1914 used to fall as low as 2 or 3 per cent. Explanation and solution is thus required of three serious developments in unemployment during the inter-war period: more violent trade cycle fluctuation; depressed areas; and perhaps in addition a generally declining trend in activity which leaves a hard and possibly hardening core of unemployment. The core consists to some extent, though not entirely, in workers who have been continuously unemployed for a long time—a hard core of unemployed. Even in the prosperous year 1937 a quarter of the unemployed in Britain had been out of work over a year. The core of unemployment may indeed be largely the result of immobility. The years 1921-1938 were unusual in causes for "frictional" unemployment when labour and industrial organization were too "sticky" to adjust themselves to rapidly changing demand. Demands for labour certainly fell rapidly after 1921, first in the industries catering for war and then in the export trades, and may not have risen with corresponding rapidity in trades exploiting new inventions such as the motor-car and electrical apparatus, and in service and distribution industries. Labour moved relatively slowly—partly owing to housing shortages, partly to the distance in location of declining and growing industries and partly perhaps owing to the palliative of unemployment insurance. It is possible too, that with the greater standards of speed, of care and of teamwork required in modern types of industry, workers comparatively incapable and unwilling to adjust themselves may be less worth employing.

The next chapter, dealing with the prevention of unemployment in the future, cannot assume "friction" to present merely a temporary problem. While pointing to ways and means of smoothing out fluctuations in trade, especially cyclical, we must allow for technological progress and changes in the demand for labour and must hope that labour and management will be more able and willing to adjust themselves than in the period 1921-37. But there always remains the possibility that this progress may be slowed down by inadjustable and sticky labour and industrial organization—whether capitalist or not—leaving a hard and hardening core of permanent unemployment. In this respect unemployment is a problem in stimulus and incentive much like the problem already tackled of inefficient employment.

CHAPTER XII

THE PREVENTION OF UNEMPLOYMENT

§1 UNDERLYING CONDITIONS OF UNEMPLOYMENT

MANY of the conditions underlying the various forms of unemployment described in the previous chapter are obviously natural or technical and not due directly to the form of control of industry. Seasonal variation in the weather affecting building operations or affecting the domestic demand for coal can hardly be attributed to capitalism; and, whatever the system of control, progress and reduction in cost of production are bound to incur some risk of technological unemployment. Moreover, certain devices such as money and the charging of prices are common to capitalism and to other systems such as the Soviet communism. Analysis of conditions underlying unemployment with its prevention in view must therefore distinguish conditions that can be changed (either by changing the form of industrial control or otherwise), and conditions which cannot be changed without losing more than was gained.

The "free" capitalist economic system shows at least six essential features: Production (i) by the help of capital equipment; (ii) in anticipation of demand; (iii) expressed in money prices addressed (iv) to the purse of *any* consumer (v) by *any* producer (vi) in search of profits. Of these six features only the last three are distinctive of capitalism. Russia, under Soviet communism, is building up large capital equipment and anticipates at least some demand expressed in money, i.e., expects to sell products for a price; but sales at various prices may be restricted to certain classes of consumers, large-scale production is by the State, and not necessarily for profits.

Since Russia continues (in spite of her reaction from capitalism) to build up equipment, anticipate demand and use a price system, we may assume that if efficiency and progress are to be maintained, these features of our own economic system cannot be changed as a remedy for unemployment. It

169

is not practical policy in a free society (and is perhaps a con-
tradiction in terms) to force consumers to a fixed schedule of
what they shall eat or wear. Rationing, as we know it, is merely
setting maximum limits to certain forms of consumption and
outside this there is still room for consumer's freedom of
choice. But it is a choice likely (especially as income rises) to
threaten full employment with unpredictable fashions, individual vagaries instead of standardization, and with a demand
for wants (often artificially stimulated by advertisement),
rather than for real needs.

Freedom of consumers' demand, freedom to produce, and
the profit motive are left, then, as conditions to be considered
in planning full employment. The freedom of anyone to set up,
invest in and own a business along any line of production or
service where he may see a chance of profit would probably
prove the most startling feature of capitalism to visitors from
another age or even from Russia to-day. For free private enterprise was not allowed in the Middle Ages with its guild regulations, and was only introduced into Western Civilization fairly
recently. As the doctrine of *laissez faire* slowly spread in the
eighteenth and nineteenth centuries, the conservatives resisting
it, thought of it as chaos; and such a free system is only
saved from a chaos (where producers would set up to make
things which nobody wanted or which everybody had too much
of already) by the profit motive—that is, the expectation of a
price above cost. Producers making goods not in demand incur
a loss and either go bankrupt or mend their ways; producers
meeting demands and meeting them at a cost below the demand
price, obtain a profit and extend their production.

This is the classical justification for the profit system, but
from the standpoint of employment, the system has several
disadvantages:

1. "Any" producer may be ignorant and unintelligent and
though either or both qualities may eventually take him out
of business, this trial and error leads by its "error" to the
unemployment of workers. The enterprise may be started at
the wrong time or place for success. In timing, the producer
may be relying on a limited memory without attempting to

forecast demand, or possibly just moved by herd-instinct. The place may be correct for the time being, but not correct over the whole life of the plant and many a factory is now incorrectly located for full employment because its builder did not look far enough ahead. Whatever the cause, there is evidence of high mortality and particularly infant mortality among private businesses, with consequence loss of employment.

2. Any private producer may calculate intelligently on accurate information so as to obtain a sufficient profit, but this profit may not lead in the direction of full and stable employment. Localization of industry and the risk of over-specialization of any one locality arises mainly because it pays the entrepreneur to go where similar entrepreneurs already are. Often, too, an entrepreneur may avoid losses if he closes down his operations partially or wholly; but the loss to the community from the consequent unemployment both in insurance benefits and loss of efficiency may be much greater than the entrepreneur's balance of gain by closing down. The individual cost and the individual gain of the private producer do not tally necessarily with public social gains, or social costs, such as full employment, or unemployment.

3. There may be too many private producers, even though they are well informed and intelligent. Larger firms and factories are in most technically developed industries probably more efficient than smaller sizes. The multiplication of firms may make the average trade transacted by one firm too small for efficiency[1] and profit and thus, under the profit system, tends to check employment.

Losses by competition in various industries may eventually bring on the later phase of capitalism often known as finance or monopoly capitalism. The efficiency of large-scale organization may spur entrepreneurs to knock one another out by alleged or genuinely unfair "cut-throat" competition, or else to "get together" in various ways. There may be complete merger of firms, permanent combines, such as the holding company, or temporary associations—all of them seeking to increase profits (or turn losses into profits) either by reduction of cost, or maintaining or raising prices, or both. To raise prices

[1] *See* Florence, *Investment, Location and Size of Plant.*

some approach to monopoly is required, but costs can often be reduced simply by larger-scale transactions, whether involving monopoly or not. The management of these larger-scale mergers, holding companies or associations has not quite the same profit incentive to enterprise as the original owner-manager entrepreneur, and arguments based on owner-managership should not be unthinkingly transferred to them. Holding companies, since they hold the stock of other companies, involve by definition the existence of joint stock companies; and mergers (and indeed any large organization requiring much capital) must almost of necessity be joint stock companies. In these companies there has often been a managerial revolution; the key men in actual control are not always the chief shareholders, but may be the directors or the general manager with little or no stock invested,[1] paid not by profit but by salary.

In short, among joint stock companies the strong incentive to efficiency and enterprise constituted by profit goes not to the key men but, in the form of dividend, to the shareholders, the great majority of whom take no active part in the control. The key men are usually paid a fixed time-rate fee or salary. It is certainly a question which should be further investigated, whether the hard-core unemployment and the slowing up of trade apparent in 1921-39 and referred to in the last chapter, was not due to the new forms of industrial organization, including the probable growth in monopolistic cartels and combines. A body of theory on the effects of imperfect competition which may throw light on this possible trend is being developed.[2]

It has been necessary to draw attention to the nature and position of the producer in the modern, and perhaps not-so-free, capitalist society, because it is on his behaviour that the newer theories of unemployment turn. These theories will now be examined.

§2 THE ROLE OF INVESTMENT

The change in economic thought brought about by Keynes'

[1] See Florence, "The Statistical Analysis of Joint Stock Company Control," *Statistical Journal*, 1947, part I.

[2] E.g., Joan Robinson, *Economics of Imperfect Competition*; J. Meade, *Economic Analysis and Policy*. See list of books, p. 223-4.

General Theory of Employment directs attention to the entre-preneur as the initiator of developments that will result in different levels of employment. Now the entrepreneur is a shorthand expression of economists for the "controlling interest" in a producing organization—the key man or men—and in the real world may mean any sole trader, a partner, the Board of Directors of a Joint Stock Company or any of its members, the Management of a Co-operative Society, a trading department of a local authority, or the controlling board of a nationalized undertaking. Which of these alternate forms the entrepreneur assumes, makes (as already suggested) more difference upon policy than abstract economists perhaps allow for, but for the present we must follow the basic analysis of the Keynes' school.

The total volume of employment is determined by the community's total spending or outlay. If more employment is wanted, additional outlay sets up a virtuous circle in immediate and derived demands for labour, which counteracts the vicious circle of the trade cycle described in the last chapter. Goods are bought and workers and managers employed at wages, salaries or profits; part of their incomes is spent on consumers' goods and thus employ additional workers and managers in consumers' goods industries; part of whose incomes in turn is spent on additional consumers' goods and so on. There is thus a "multiplier" whereby any increase in outlay will indirectly involve more in total outlay; how much more will depend on how far recipients of the extra income from the additional outlay "lay it out" in turn, rather than saving it. Outlay is incurred either by private persons and industrial organizations or by the State, either for purposes of consumption or of investment. Consumption is not in normal times increased at all readily by private persons on average. Increases of income are usually saved rather than consumed since the average consumer has a fairly fixed mode and standard of living. He will not increase his spending to an extent commensurate with increased income and the surplus income is thus saved auto-matically. This diminishing "marginal" propensity to consume can be verified from family budgets, where the higher income families are found on average to have a considerably higher proportion of income not spent than the families with lower incomes.

The failure to spend income, i.e. "saving," is not automatically related to capital investment (or, to use less confusing words, to "equipping" and "stocking"), as the classical economists thought. Possible savers and those responsible for capital equipment, i.e., the entrepreneurs, are usually different people. If people save and there is no equivalent investment, total outlay falls and with it the numbers employed until a new level is reached, where reduced national income reduces the saving.

To keep up total outlay and avoid unemployment reliance cannot be placed on private consumption and recourse must be had either to private investment or to outlay by the State. Private persons are limited in the ways they can invest in equipment and stocks out of their own savings, so that (apart from State outlay) the questions now arise, what will cause the private industrial organizations (capitalist or co-operative) to invest more or to invest less in equipment and stock and thus to stimulate or restrict employment, and why the process of investment in equipment and stock fails at certain times?

Under the capitalist system enterprise in extending production in any direction depends on expectation of a series of annual profits to the capitalist. This profit income must be greater than interest on a safe long-term security, for if a capitalist entrepreneur could get no more income from his capital than that interest, he would buy safe securities like Government stock. Capitalist enterprise in any direction therefore depends in theory on the expected series of returns to the additional capital goods compared to the expected rate of interest. "In theory" is inserted because, in fact, the capitalist usually takes the rate of interest for granted and concentrates attention on fluctuations in the value of his returns, particularly those caused by price changes. Price changes may be serious, for if (while his goods are in production) prices fall, the capitalist finds that he has bought stock and perhaps equipment at high prices, but will have to sell their product at the new lower price level.

Over and above the vagaries of the consumer whose demand he is anticipating, investment (equipping and stocking) by the capitalist entrepreneur is thus fraught with uncertainty. The equipment the entrepreneur must buy will, as a result of modern technical advance, have to anticipate demand some way ahead, and will be expensive, soon obsolescent and probably specialized. There will be a high constant depreciation cost, however low the output, and the entrepreneur will not readily be able to switch from one type of output to another if the demands of the consumers are not as anticipated. Moreover, even if *total* demand is gauged accurately competitors may make the total supply being produced to meet the demand (and thus the share left to any one competitor) difficult to gauge. In short, the uncertainties of profit under modern conditions present the possibility of private enterprise and investment for profits, distinctive of the capitalist system, drying up at least at certain times. Spare resources held by an entrepreneur may simply be kept liquid at the bank or in Government securities to earn interest, and not be invested in industrial equipment or stock, and may therefore fail to maintain employment.

Though possibly significant for the hardening core of unemployment, attention has been called to private investment policy by contemporary economists less as explaining general trends and hard-core unemployment, than in explanation of the violence of the trade cycle. Prosperity may, as already shown, bring higher labour costs such as turnover and absenteeism. And after a certain period of business confidence, during which capital stocks and equipment have been accumulating, the extra profit to be got out of extra "marginal" amounts of capital is likely to be less. Since equipment and most stocks are durable, part of the total of capital goods in existence will become redundant.

"The competition of each new arrival reduces the level of profits for those already in existence. The expansion of investment slows down. . . . Once investment begins to decline, the multiplier is set to work in the downward direction, consumption falls off, unemployment increases, and activity and profits decline. The prospects of future profits degenerate under the influence of their present decline, investment falls still further, and the downward movement feeds on itself."[1]

[1]Joan Robinson, *Introduction to the Theory of Employment*, Chapter XII.

This vicious circle of unemployment whose action on labour was described in the previous chapter is accentuated by the quasi-herd instinct of the typical modern capitalist. Again attention must be paid to the prevailing type of entrepreneur. The capitalist form is no longer identical with an independent-minded owner-manager but consists normally of the directors, managers and shareholders (mostly divorced from management) of a joint stock company. Investment in new issues which, with profits ploughed back, form the main finance for new capital, depend on the mood of ignorant shareholders; a mood based on fleeting, contemporary events such as the trade cycle and influenced by short-term speculation on the Stock Exchange (looking for profit from quick resale of their purchase) rather than by genuine long-term expectation of profitability.[1]

§3 THE POLICY OF SECURITY AND FULL EMPLOYMENT

Owing to technical advance and institutional changes in the prevailing type of entrepreneur, some anxiety is thus clearly justified about the incentive power of prospective profits on capital investment, in relation to rates of interest and the preference for "liquid" assets. There is likely to be insufficient investment by private (including co-operative) entrepreneurs to employ all the time of all persons able and willing to work. Recourse must be had to public outlay for consumption or for investment in capital equipment. Since in peace time investment involves bigger variations in outlay than consumption, the public entrepreneur must enter the field particularly to supply the capital the capitalist system fails to supply, and thus to avoid both trade cycles and declining trends.

The official White Paper on Employment Policy (1944, Cmd. 6527) proposes that "public investment both in timing and in volume must be carefully planned to offset fluctuations in private investment"; others, notably Lord Beveridge, would substitute for a merely offsetting policy, a general policy of public control of investment which would include within its purview private investment and budgetary deficits.[2] Both official and unofficial plans, however, stress the importance of location of industry as well as the timing of investment.

[1]*See* Keynes, *General Theory of Employment,* 1936, Chapter XII.
[2]*See* Beveridge, *Full Employment in a Free Society.*

The essence of planning against unemployment may indeed be expressed as timing and placing. Timing presupposes a series of plans kept (as President Roosevelt's Planning Board put it) like "blue-prints on the shelf," ready to be put into execution as unemployment appears to threaten. Three stages in planning public works are thus envisaged. First a social and economic survey of the needs of the country as a whole or of any region or town such as the West Midlands or Worcester.[1] Secondly, detailed paper plans to meet these needs, drawn up by an architect or surveyor. Finally, and not till such time as unemployment of men and resources threatens, the execution of the plan.

"Placing" industrial activity to prevent unemployment is largely a policy of local diversification. Seasonal industries should be placed together, whose fluctuations "dovetail" into one another, summer-slack with winter-slack industries. Industries subject to cyclical fluctuations should be "braced" with cyclically stable industries declining industries "spliced" with growing industries. In the past the profit motive of the capitalist entrepreneur has led away from diversification, and there has been sharp localization of many manufacturing industries. Localization has many economic advantages which, if overridden, will raise costs[2] and may well reduce the competitive strength of a country in international competition; nor does it follow that all industrial localization involves "one-industry" towns. If a town is large enough, it may (like Birmingham) contain several localized industries, but to a smaller town the localization of an industry (like carpets at Kidderminster or pottery at Stoke) may involve specialization and "all eggs in one basket."

The outstanding examples of the dangers of such specialization were the distressed industrial areas of South Wales, the North East coast and Clydeside mentioned in the last chapter. A diversification policy must not aim at putting a bit of every industry into every town, but at finding those towns which specialize in industries where there is risk of unemployment

[1] E.g., Glaisyer, Brennan, Ritchie and Florence, *County Town.* West Midland Group, *Conurbation.*
[2] Florence, *Investment, Location and Size of Plant,* 1947, pp. 51 ff.

and in adding a few carefully selected industries. Industries vary in their mobility, that is in the economic feasibility of placing and planning them at will, and may be classified and labelled accordingly as rooted, tied, linked and footloose.

"There are extractive industries like mining and agriculture rooted to natural resources, and semi-extractive industries like iron smelting, rooted for practical purposes by the cost of transport of one of their raw materials. There are other industries tied to their market by the cost of transport of their product including the residentiary industries tied to the consumer market and linked industries tied to some other industry as market, yet there remain many industries that are mobile or footloose which would be free from rooting or tying."[1]

Among footloose industries the principle of selection should be a diagnosis of the existing local industrial structure, and search for industries with characteristics that will dovetail, brace and splice with existing industries and generally secure against the local risks. If, as in the depressed areas, the locality suffers from cyclical slumps, declining trends and insufficient occupation for women, industries should be introduced that are cyclically stable, growing in trend, and employ women in high proportion. Different remedies will be required in different situations such as the countryside specializing in agriculture[2] or a port importing heavy materials. The industries introduced while counteracting the disease should not themselves be economically unfitted for the new site or, by leaving, create unemployment in their original site. Light metal industries cyclically stable, growing, and employing women, but requiring skilled craftsmen, should not be moved from areas where they are closely linked with other industries (e.g., supplying parts or performing necessary processing or servicing) into areas where they will find little linkage and no skilled craftsmen. Careful industrial analysis of the area of threatened unemployment which is to be developed; of the industries proposed for

[1]Glaisyer, Brennan, Ritchie and Florence, *County Town*, 1946, pp. 83-4. A whole chapter (IV) is devoted to the problems of Industrial Location.

[2]*See* Florence, "The Selection of Industries Suitable for Dispersion into Rural Areas," *Statistical Journal*, 1944, Part II.

introduction; and of the area where these industries would otherwise have grown, should succeed in discovering branches of industry suitable for a "planning" manoeuvre. This does not imply any moving of factories physically, but plans for diverting any proposed new factory from the old location of its industry to the development area.

The implementation by the Government of plans for diversification need not be described here any more than the details of methods of public control over investment. As far as they affect labour, however, plans for diversification must not be looked upon as a substitute for mobility. Not all industries can come to the unemployed or unoccupied worker, and many workers must still be prepared to go to the industry. Inter-industrial movement must also occur, even though physical movement to a new home is not required. To be effective against unemployment, diversification assumes that workers will move freely from one to another of the diverse industries in the same place. It assumes, for instance, that some workers attached to a winter-peak trade will move in summer to a summer-peak trade in the same area. A similar assumption underlies schemes for decasualization. The essence of decasualization is to diminish the numbers casually attached to a trade and form a consistently attached nucleus with guaranteed wage if work fails. Many casual workers will thus lose even their casual earnings and are expected to move into other trades. How far these assumptions or expectations are correct will be discussed in the next section with particular reference to full employment policies.

§4 Full Employment, Mobility and Efficiency

The target for full employment admits a certain low proportion of unemployment owing to changes in technique, seasonal variations and uncertainties of foreign trade. To workers out of work for these, or any other reasons, benefit is to be paid. The full plan of security against unemployment is thus to prevent it by increased outlay, especially investment, carefully timed and placed, and (where it cannot be prevented) to offer palliatives for the loss of wages.

The incidence of unemployment, so far as it is not technological, was analysed in the previous chapter as one of persons, time, place or particular industries. The full employment policy is aimed particularly at smoothing out time and place variations. The plan involves dangers, however, of retarding development as between different industries and of neglecting personal differences in efficiency.

In the period 1923-37 industries deviated widely in their development. Electrical apparatus doubled its employment as Table 17 shows, while in the cotton industry employment fell by a sixth. Similar, if not wider, deviations must be expected in the future and mobility of labour from the declining to the expanding industries must be stimulated. Stimulation of mobility, like that of efficiency, must be addressed both to capacity and willingness.

Capacity to move from one industry or occupation to another depends upon general education which usually makes the mind more adjustable, and specific training for the new job. The Beveridge proposals included compulsion (after drawing six months unemployment benefit) to attend training courses and official schemes include a similar provision. Movement from job to job is helped if different industries are found located in the same area, so that the worker is not required to move geographically as well as industrially or occupationally. This facilitation of industrial mobility is one aspect of the diversification of an area's industries, and since different industries often repeat the same occupations (such as toolmakers or general labourers or clerks) a worker can change industries in a town of many industries without either changing his home or his occupation. If such towns contain several localized industries, however, they are likely to be large and to constitute congested areas.

Capacity to move geographically depends obviously on ability to pay cost of transport. During the period of heavy unemployment before the last war, the cost of travel to a new job (duly secured through an Employment Exchange) was paid by the Government under the transference policy. But now, after the war, lack of housing is a more serious obstacle.

Unwillingness to move from one industry to another or from place to place is partly economic, partly psychological.

Unless the worker receives lower earnings or has a lower status in his new job, change of job within the same place may not raise unsurmountable unwillingness. Where both job and place are changed, however, the worker is not in an economic position to take risks and must be certain of securing a job at a satisfactory wage in the new place. Information on this score can be provided by the chain of employment exchanges set up over the whole country. Furthermore, workers normally move in families. This "convention" means that all earners in the family must find jobs in the new place. The father, even if unemployed, would be unwilling to move to another town if his son or his daughter who was earning good money in the home town were to find no source of income in the new. The total family income might well be reduced. Even if the family were "unconventionally" split, payment to landladies might easily mop up the difference of wages over unemployment benefit.

Unwillingness to move often has a psychological and sociological basis, independent of economic reasoning. The extreme case, that of emigrating abroad with total change of language, habits, friends, points to the obstacles. To many a Welshman, moving perhaps only to Birmingham, eighty miles away, is like moving abroad. Care must be taken therefore that the economic motive to move is not so weakened as to fail in overcoming the conventional and psychological factors and the force of habit. Palliative payments must not be so nearly equal to wages that palliation is preferred to prevention—benefits in unemployment at home preferred to wages in employment elsewhere.

Unlike efficiency, mobility is only required of a fringe of workers since in peace time demand changes only slowly. One solution is to catch young workers before they are encumbered by family ties and the force of habit. For changes in the man-power of different industries can be affected not only by changing over existing personnel, but by tapping the original source of young recruits. Every year boys and girls enter industry on leaving school partly replacing workers who have died or retired. This stream of recruits can be fairly willingly guided into various industries or occupations at least in the home town. So that, apart from geographical mobility with its family-unit obstacles, the vocational guidance described in Chapter IX in which school, employment exchanges and employers co-operate, must be brought into the service of adjusting labour supply to changes in the type of demands upon labour.

The plan for full employment must, then, include precautions for ensuring mobility between industries and occupations. The plan must, however, also ensure that full employment does not lower incentives to efficiency *on the job*.

Two danger points arise from the preventive and palliative measures included in the plan. If full employment means more jobs than men (*a*) dismissal for inefficiency is less likely, and fear of it may not exist to act as a spur to efficiency on the job; and (*b*) workers may be continually quitting to seek for other jobs in their own trade thus raising the costly labour turnover rate. Unless they are moving from a less to a more efficient organization they are not necessarily conferring any benefit on the nation by such mobility. Mobility is not good in itself; it is an advantage only when the labour force thereby adjusts itself to changes in consumers' demands and to the relative efficiency of producers. The danger is that full employment policies while obstructing this adjustment may encourage "functionless" mobility which merely raises the labour cost of factory or firm.

In minimizing the threat of these danger points it is often said that inefficiency coupled with security from dismissal, and persistent turnover applies only to a minority of workers. This is no doubt true; but if a large national output is required the minority must be efficient as well as the majority and the minority may be quite a large one. Its size is a matter of investigation and, indeed, the problems consequent upon the full employment of every worker require as much research and informed "know-how" in their solutions as the allied problems of full efficiency of the average worker. Otherwise full employment may merely mean a fall in average efficiency.

PART IV

THE DIRECTION OF LABOUR POLICY

CHAPTER XIII

THE CONTROL OF LABOUR CONDITIONS

§1 THE EMPLOYER LET ALONE

CONCLUSIONS were reached in Parts II and III as to the conditions causing the inefficient employment and the unemployment of labour. By altering and controlling these conditions inefficiency and unemployment can be prevented or reduced. The question now arises, who is to be charged with the required alteration and control of conditions?

In the early stage of the industrial revolution the answer was sure. The dominant theory of economics and politics was that of *laissez faire*, literally of letting the private individual make what he liked. This policy of freedom for enterprise was extended to freedom of contract—of letting the bargain between the employer and the employed worker be what they liked. The function of the State was merely to "keep the ring": to see that a few employers did not abuse their freedom and break the rules by paying workers in "truck" rather than money, or by breaking contracts more specifically. This freedom of contract, it was held, would result in the greatest wealth of the greatest number since each individual knew best his own interests and his interest would guide him where his labour was most wanted. If the demand of the employers for labour outran supply in any industry, they would offer higher wages and thus attract a greater supply. Conversely, if the supply of labour outran demand, there would be unemployment or lower wages, and labour would be deterred from that industry by starvation. *Laissez faire* political economy took a wide national, if not international view in which the total of wealth, progress and mobility of labour to meet rapidly changing technical conditions was the prime consideration. It did not envisage all-round or long-term unemployment and worried little about efficiency within a firm, but assumed that with free trade, free competition and labour free to turn over, inefficient firms unable to pay the normal level of wages would go out of business. Though the tendency to over-population would always keep wages down, labour conditions would at least be better than State or trade union interference with "freedom" could achieve.

Unfortunately for the *laissez faire* case, the period in which it flourished and was applied as State (or rather State-less) policy was one of acute industrial misery. One function that the Government still retained in Britain, though not usually mentioned, was important in disclosing this failure—the function of making investigations. Official observation of the facts showed by induction that deductive speculation had miscalculated. Select Committees of Parliament, Reports of Inspectors and Public Health Officers, Statistical Blue Books and Royal Commissions all pointed to abject poverty and low wages, the ravages of disease, and working practices which shocked public opinion. These State documents were the material on which Engels and Marx based much of their indictment of the capitalist·system; in the index of Marx's *Das Kapital*, Vol. I, there are more references to British Parliamentary Papers than to any other source of information. These inquiries led to legislation like the Mines Act, regulating and limiting individual contracts between employers and workers—beginning with children and then young persons and women. *Laissez faire* came gradually to be abandoned.

If shorter hours, higher wages and expenditure on improving other conditions often leads eventually to an increase in labour efficiency which may repay the employer, as we have shown in Part II, why did enlightened employers under the regime of *laissez faire* not spontaneously adopt such policies?

In the early phase of the industrial revolution the bulk of firms were small in financial resources and highly competitive, and usually could not afford to take the long view. Money efficency conditions which might eventually bear fruit in labour penits on would at first have to be recouped from price; but to charge a higher price than less far-seeing competitors meant loss of markets and ruin before labour efficiency ripened. The entrepreneur was thus forced to be an unenlightened economic man, automatically, by sheer force of circumstances. In any case, the majority of entrepreneurs were not by nature enlightened economic men. They were not in business "for their health," much less their employees' health. Profits were the difference between receipts and costs, and wages the greater part of the costs. Increasing wages and improving labour conditions, to their minds, just reduced profit. Few of them cared to inquire, like Owen and later Lord Brassey, whether increased wages did not result in greater output and efficiency and thus greater receipts and profits. The employers in practice took the class struggle for granted and had little incentive to make further inquiry. Thanks to a high birth rate, maintained up till 1878, and a fall in death rates, supplies of labour were plentiful. If disease or death overtook his hands, the employer could easily replace them. It was a policy of "hire and fire."

The bargaining position of labour was, in fact, so much weaker than the position of the employer that his liberty of contract, held so sacred by the *laissez faire* philosophy, seldom materialized. No one has put the reasons more clearly than an economist, Professor Alfred Marshall. He pointed out that since most employers have several employees, workers are more numerous and thus open to more severe competition than employers and that workers without dependents could undercut the worker paterfamilias. Moreover workers were poorer than employers and their labour power perishable, there were no reserves to fall back on if they refused the terms offered; and in the actual tactics and strategy of bargaining, workers were not experienced like the entrepreneur whose whole life was one of bargaining, nor had they the necessary knowledge of the trade position. (The next section will show how the organization of trade unions overcame these handicaps in labour's position, without the aid of the State.) In any case, children, employed from the age of five onward, could hardly be expected to exercise their freedom of contract with much discretion, nor could they be expected to form trade unions. Here the *laissez faire* school admitted the exception where the

State must interfere, and the earliest factory legislation was to limit the hours of older children and to prohibit the employment of younger children entirely. This development of protective State policy will be discussed in §4.

The main stream of capitalism has changed considerably since the era of pure, almost Stateless, *laissez faire*. The bulk of manufactures no longer comes from small, highly competitive workshops controlled by an entrepreneur working for a profit and owning his own capital. It comes instead from large factories owned by joint stock companies and controlled by boards of directors with general managers, paid mainly by salary not profit. The general manager or managing director is assisted by departmental managers for sales, for production (the works manager) and sometimes for labour (frequently known as the personnel manager). The works department often has a planning section, and the personnel department sections dealing with wages, health and safety, training and employment. The men in charge of employment conditions are specialists and they must often co-operate with representatives of labour. The initiative still lies with the employer, usually through his planning department, in determining the physical lay-out of the plant and the technical processes and type of production, and also in settling speeds and piece rates and carrying out time and motion study and any scientific management there may be. Beyond these physical matters the employer's control is more limited both in scope and function. The personnel department, besides carrying out the preventive and curative welfare and safety work described in Chapter VI, selects, trains, and occasionally dismisses workers, and usually keeps records of absenteeism and labour turnover.

Apart from supervisory and recording functions, independent executive action on labour by the employer thus tends to be confined to the number and identity of workers to be employed. Executive personnel functions are to-day usually a matter of adjusting general policies agreed upon with the workers or commanded by the State, or of co-operating in joint consultations. The enlightened employer with a welfare policy can adjust hours below, or wages above agreed rates; he can put in rest pauses or pay special bonuses above basic minima; but he cannot on his own settle basic wages or hours. Here he must jointly consult with and take orders from other parties in the employment relationship such as the workers (represented by trade unions or on works councils) or the State. Quite apart from the growth in powers of industrial control of these parties (traced in the following pages), workers are inclined to take the enlightened model employer acting on his own as too paternalistic.

The gradual change-over in methods of implementing labour policies from that of the isolated employer to joint action may no doubt be explained by the average employer's lack of care for labour conditions. Robert Owen's appeal quoted in Chapter II never became out of date, but "care" has two shades of meaning. When the employer was an entrepreneur living by profit and with little capital equipment, he had a direct incentive to higgle down labour; his lack of care was deliberate, and deliberately careful and model entrepreneurs like Owen himself, in spite of their evident prosperity, failed to serve as a model to others—in fact, were considered by their fellow entrepreneurs as freaks. But with the predominance of highly capitalized joint-stock companies and salaried managers a second phase opened. Lack of care became less a deliberate attitude and more a consequence of circumstances, particularly the managers' pre-occupation with aspects of industrial policy other than labour.

The main problems of top control on which managers concentrated were what and how much of it to produce, at what price and how far to mechanize. Labour conditions and terms of employment have to them been a subsidiary matter—merely one of many costs to be subtracted from gross receipts before profit could be declared. The costs of mistakes in labour policy have often been less important to profit than the price of materials or (if the factory was highly mechanized) than the cost of machines and equipment. In consequence the majority even of large-scale managers are little more conversant than the small entrepreneur with the findings of industrial psychology and physiology.

With full employment and labour shortage and growing nationalization of industries, a third phase may now be opening up in management's attitude to labour. Getting and keeping efficient labour is no longer a subsidiary consideration and the trade union and State control over conditions may well be found too negative—a series of *"don'ts"*. Implementing the conclusions of industrial psychology is not just a matter of "don't work longer than x hours or don't pay less than y wages". It is a positive policy of selecting and promoting suitable individuals and types, training and giving them incentives under conditions making for efficiency. In future the employer may have to acquire a deeper knowledge of the human factor and jointly with the worker and the State assume a more active part in the implementation of that knowledge.

§2 WORKERS' CONTROL

If the employer could not be relied upon single-handed for an enlightened adjustment and control of the conditions of labour, what other party could be called in to the task of implementation? An answer, which in the past had a wide appeal, is labour itself. "Workers' Control" has been advocated by Syndicalists and the National Guild or Guild-Socialist movement to cover control of all industrial policy. Here the issue is how and under what labour conditions to produce; not the ultimate control (envisaged by syndicalists) which determines amounts and kinds of products and their price. The contention that labour should itself control labour conditions is strong, since no one better than labour can tell where the shoe pinches.

At the outset of the industrial revolution the shoe pinched chiefly because in bargaining with the employer about terms of employment, labour was (due to causes already given) in a weaker bargaining position. These causes could be, and were, offset by collective action. A trade union built up reserve funds, represented the numerous workers as one body, and employed as a paid secretary a full-time skilled bargainer able to acquire knowledge of trade conditions. The workers' relative weakness was only offset gradually and piecemeal by efficient organization, beginning with certain skilled crafts in certain towns, and this development from sporadic points is still reflected in the low proportion of trade union members among the black-coated salariat, farm labourers, and women workers, and in a certain lack of co-ordination between trade unions. Craft and industrial unions cut across one another's membership and general unions have grown up prepared to accept almost all workers.

The majority of workers in mining, transport, building and many manufactures are now in trade unions; the Trade Union Congress imposes a certain co-ordination; and in a large sector of industry, trade unions are sufficiently organized to redress all bargaining weakness and to give workers some chance of controlling their terms of employment.

Judging from the objects of strikes, the terms workers are keenest to control are their wages, and particularly (by minimum guaranteed wages) their financial security. In cotton, printing, the boot and shoe, and other industries, whole price lists of piece wages are collectively agreed upon. In yet other industries, such as engineering, a basic wage for different grades is usually the aim of the trade union, with bonus additions or sliding scales, as explained in Chapter VIII.

Hours of work are, next to wages, the greatest concern of trade unions. The two are connected, since the maximum hours fixed by agreement with trade unions can be exceeded if the employer is prepared to pay time and a half, or occasionally, as on Sundays, double time for the overtime hours worked.

Control over physical and social working conditions and selection is also involved in trade union action when, as sometimes occurs, it takes the form of demanding the removal of an unpopular foreman or the reinstatement of a worker or, as in mines, the improvement of safety conditions. The policy of the closed shop, i.e., closed to non-unionists, also implies labour control over the selection of workers, but the policy is supported more by feelings of injustice when non-strikers taking no risks get the benefits secured by trade unionists who did risk a strike, rather than by a desire for greater control.

To help their bargaining position on direct issues (such as wages) it is often necessary to control (according to orthodox economic teaching) certain determining factors, like the demand and supply of labour. So, through their trade unions workers also try to control, by limiting apprentices, the supply of labour to skilled trades; and try to fix demand by a "demarcation" of the work a skilled man should do, and by opposing any "dilution" by the unskilled.

What are the means used by trade unions to secure these ultimate and immediate terms of employment? Clearly, a stable structure has to be built up to meet the employers in negotiation. As soon as equality with the employers' bargaining position is approached and the workers are no longer a subject people, the parallel between diplomacy (and possibly war) between nations, and the industrial relations between the trade union structure and employers is difficult to resist. Of the four methods which are used by trade unions in their relation to the employers, two (mutual insurance and political action) are calculated to strengthen the structure of trade unions. One, collective bargaining, is diplomacy and treaty making, and the other, the strike, is warfare.

All other methods for gaining the aims of trade unions are subsidiary to collective bargaining. Mutual insurance, offering superannuation and incapacity benefits, and strike pay to members in return for their contributions, holds together the members of a union so that bargaining can be really collective. Political action—the voluntary levy on union members in support of "Labour" candidates—was originally undertaken to maintain by legislation the status of the funds and of the officials of trade unions, the "collective" body. The strike is by definition collective and though comparatively infrequent, as shown in Chapter III, provides the sanction without which employers would have no cause for making any concessions in the bargaining. In short, while insurance and political action support the structure of the bargaining bodies, the strike gives "teeth" to the bargaining process.

Bargaining is collective in two senses. It aims to secure maximum hours, minimum wages and other terms that apply to a whole collectivity of workers; it aims, in short, at a common rule or standardization of conditions. And the bargaining process is collective in the sense that it is conducted on behalf of a whole collectivity of workers, single individual workers or employers not doing their own bargaining.

Following closely the organization of trade unions, the actual scope of the collective bargaining is usually either an industry or an occupation (or craft) locally or nationally, not any single factory, mine or firm. Individual employers must toe the common line of minimum wages or maximum hours just like individual workers, thus preventing competitive undercutting by firms at the expense of the workers.

These rules, common to a whole occupation or industry, are, to continue the international parallel, general treaties which may have to be interpreted in particular cases. Both treaty-making and interpretation are performed by collective bargaining, but for interpretation a simplified, more economical procedure is usually adopted. The case may, in the first instance, be referred to the professional secretaries on either side before taking it up with the whole representative committee, or it may be taken up, but only locally, before appealing to the district or the national organization. This system of decentralized or delegated interpretation has made democratic joint action an economical and effective machine, through which workers can operate detailed as well as general control over wages, hours and other conditions of employment.

The particular effects of control through collective bargaining may be summed up under five heads:

(i) Conditions favouring quality rather than quantity of output are likely to be implemented since workers have a pride in their workmanship.

(ii) In the course of bargaining, comparison will be made with the terms of employment of other but similar grades of work. In discussing wages, the counter-balancing disadvantages of an occupation (detailed in Chapter VIII), such as its dirtiness or irregularity will be taken into account.

(iii) Among the "other things" they assume equal, economists usually put bargaining power and knowledge. Hence the trade unions by providing for labour equal bargaining power and knowledge which otherwise would not exist, should bring wages nearer to the results of the "free interplay" of the economic forces of supply and demand.

(iv) On the other hand, traditions which technical change may have rendered out of date are likely to be reinforced. The wages structure of any one industry, illustrated in Chapter VII, is likely to be ingrained in the minds of workers, and the same pattern will be frozen in new agreements, though the demand or supply conditions of different wage-grades may have changed radically.

(v) Moreover, if traditional terms of employment are at all changed by trade union action, changes are likely to be due not to new forces of demand and supply but to a new balance of bargaining power within an occupation or industry. A strongly unionized industry, for instance, may increase its wage rates relative to those of other industries, though its products are not increasing relatively in demand or its labour diminishing relatively in supply. As a result, labour may fail to move in response to new demands or new techniques.

This likelihood that mere collective bargaining between trade unions and employers, industry by industry, will fail to provide incentives to mobility leads to the consideration of alternative methods.

§3 STATE PARTICIPATION IN NEGOTIATION

Since the days of *laissez faire* with the State merely "keeping the ring" for the higgling between individual worker and entrepreneur, and making occasional inquiries, a regular machinery of collective negotiation has been set up for controlling conditions of employment. At first this machinery involved only workers and employers. Later the State has come to play an increasing part in the negotiations, but the procedure still retains the *laissez faire* principle that in the first instance, the interested parties—workers and employers—shall fight it out. The State will only intervene if called upon by either party as the critical decision is approached, or if one of the parties is too weak for the fight to be fair or to take place at all. The key to the intricate complications of modern industrial relations is indeed the stage *at* which, and the power *with* which the State intervenes. Only in this way will method be found in the apparent madness.

State action may be ranked as one of five degrees according to power exercised or to the stages of discussion and decision where intervention occurs.

(i) The primary basic procedure is one of no State intervention. There is collective bargaining between employers' association and trade union with usually a standing joint conciliation machinery within each industry or occupation, and possibly works councils in the single factories. Agreement on terms and conditions of employment is reached and maintained without State participation. This procedure has proved effective for wages agreements where trade unions are well organized and give the worker bargaining power more or less equal to that of the employer, as in building, iron and steel, shipbuilding, engineering, or cotton industries. Judging from statistics of the way strikes were settled and wages altered, this *laissez faire* collective bargaining was still the predominant procedure for industry as a whole in Britain for the period 1924-36. It is often combined, for wage fixing, with an automatic cost of living sliding scale.

(ii) In this basically *laissez faire* procedure, the State may intervene very mildly and indirectly by creating or encouraging the creation of a bargaining body meeting regularly on which it is not represented. The Whitley Joint Industrial Councils, for instance, consisting of employers' and workers' representatives only, are set up voluntarily by the Ministry of Labour. Once set up, the Government leaves them to act on their own and their decisions are not legally enforceable. This procedure is adopted where the workers are not quite able to organize themselves on an equal footing with the employers, as in pottery, wool and distributive trades. The original plan of the Whitley Committee was for a pyramid of joint councils in each industry numerous at works level, fewer at district level, and fewest at national level. This decentralization would have created as economical a machine as decentralized collective bargaining. Many Works Councils exist, some taking the form (encouraged by the Government during the recent war) of Production Committees, but the pyramid is incomplete at district level.

(iii) Historically preceding the setting up of Whitley Councils, but logically a step further from *laissez faire* in the degree of power the State exercises, is actual Government interposition in the course of discussion. In peace-time Britain, this form of intervention has usually to be requested by one or both of the

G

bargaining parties. In some other countries (notably Australia and New Zealand) the Government may interpose "compulsorily" without the request of either party, and time is often allowed for discussion, by compulsion to delay a strike. The bodies to whom the Government turns when called upon to interpose may be private but experienced persons chosen from a panel or officials of the Ministry of Labour, or *ad hoc* boards or industrial courts. But in all cases, these bodies represent the public interest and to that extent the State takes a hand in implementing terms of employment.

The immediate reason for Government interposition in discussion is the avoidance of a threatened strike by workers (or lock-out by employers) with its consequent costs to the workers, the employers and the community. Since the strike is the main weapon of the workers, without which their bargaining power is seldom equal to that of the employers, collective bargaining normally involves at least a threat of strike and, once they assume the responsibility of avoiding strikes, the Government must be prepared for intervention at or without the request of either party. In the course of collective negotiations, there are a number of stages at each of which deadlock and dispute may occur. There may be refusal to meet the initiating party and to investigate the facts at all. There may be deadlock during the actual debate (often due to disagreement about facts). There may be difficulty over precise formulation of the decision.[1] And the deadlock or dispute at each of these stages in bargaining may deteriorate from a grievance, to a threat of strike or lock-out, to the calling of a strike or lock-out, and strike or lock-out actually in progress.

Words that are used to describe Government interposition in one or other of these stages of bargaining, are conciliation, mediation and arbitration. Though often used loosely and sometimes almost interchangeably, it is convenient to conform to the definitions suggested by the Royal Commission on Labour of 1894, and to employ Government conciliation to

---

[1]These stages in the discussion or negotiation are named in accordance with a system applicable to democratic procedures generally. *See* Florence, *Statistical Method in Economics and Political Science*, pp. 417-18.

refer to the earlier stages of initiating discussion and to the pre-bargaining situation. By *conciliation*, the Government tries to get the two parties to meet together "with a view to amicable settlement," leaving debate and formulation of the decision to flourish in the friendly atmosphere created. In *mediation* the Government representative enters into the actual bargaining or debate stage, often taking the chair, as the word implies "in the middle of" the two contending parties. At this stage unbiased investigation is often required and the Government may organize a Court of Inquiry, but it is still using its good offices, making recommendations perhaps, but not an award. In *arbitration*, the Government intervenes in the formulation stage to decide the issue and to make an award either in conjunction with both parties or alone. If alone, both parties usually agree beforehand to accept the decision. Mediation and arbitration were in Britain voluntary, at least in peacetime, but now are under certain circumstances compulsorily enforced.

(iv) A further step away from *laissez faire* is for the State not merely to interpose itself when collective bargainers show signs of failure to agree, but for the State to participate regularly and to initiate negotiation from the very beginning about terms of employment. The British Trade Boards, now known as Wages Councils, are the outstanding case. These Boards or Councils, whose function is to fix wages rates in industries where they are compulsorily set up, have a chairman and usually two assessors appointed by the Ministry of Labour in addition to an equal number of workers' and employers' representatives. Normally these State representatives hold the balance between opposing sides and determine the final award. This award is compulsory. In fact, it appears generally that the more the Government participates in bargaining the more are bargains compulsorily enforceable. No mere State creation of organization (ii above), or intervention merely at the initiation or debate stage of bargaining (iii above) carries compulsion except perhaps to delay. Intervention at the later and more crucial stage of formulating a decision such as by arbitration may or may not carry compulsion. Direct State participation at all stages from initiation to decision definitely does carry compulsion to honour the terms of employment awarded. This all-stage participation by the State, embodied in Wages Councils, was originally adopted in "sweated industries" where wages failed to give subsistence, but has been extended to all industries in which workers were unable to acquire equal bargaining power with the employers.

The guiding principle now running through the different methods of implementing terms of employment in different industries is that the procedure adopted is in keeping with the bargaining strength of the workers. Strongly organized industries are left to act on their own; weakly organized industries have bargaining organs created for them; unorganized and perhaps unorganizable industries have full Government intervention. They include (under the old Trade Boards) tailoring trades and milk roundsmen; under the special Wages Boards, agriculture; and under the new Wages Councils, retailing.

(v) Finally, there may be no bargaining by industry at all; the State simply lays down specific regulations by legislation which are enforced by inspectors and the law courts.

§4 RESORT TO STATE REGULATION

Action by the State to change the terms of employment without workers or employers participating is logically at the opposite pole to *laissez faire*, under which the interested parties should have the main say in controlling their own affairs. State regulation would be expected historically to have been introduced last in the retreat from *laissez faire*, but this has not been the case. In Britain, as early as 1802, maximum hours were laid down by legislation for pauper apprentices, and in 1819 all children under nine were prohibited by law from working in cotton mills and under sixteen from working more than twelve hours a day. *Laissez faire* was never a dogma to be applied to all cases. It rested on the apparently reasonable assumption that most persons understood their interests and knew what was good for them, and exceptions were always admitted in children. *Laissez faire* rested also on the less reasonable assumption that people who understood their own interests and what was good for them, were able to get it. Admitted exceptions are here more numerous, include adults unable to form trade unions, and justify the introduction of Wages Councils where-ever collective bargaining on an equal footing proved impossible.

The attitude to *laissez faire* to-day is rather like that of English law to an accused person. It is considered innocent unless explicitly proved guilty. The gradually increasing deviation from the *laissez faire* doctrine in implementing changes in term of employment, described in the successive sections of this chapter can all be explicitly justified. The employer could not be let alone because the workers, even if they knew what was good for them, could not singly get it against the employers' superior bargaining power. Collective bargaining between employers and workers organized in trade unions could not be let alone without State participation because it entailed losses by strikes. Finally collective bargaining even with State participation could not be let alone because, where young persons were concerned, they did not know what was good for them.

The philosophy of *laissez faire* still underlies, however, the implementation of changes in the terms of employment for the prevention of labour inefficiency. The classical philosophy of the least possible State intervention is indeed reinforced by modern conceptions of administration. Thus Mary Follett speaks of conciliation as a more satisfactory way of settling industrial disputes than arbitration, because it allows for a process of interchange of ideas between the two sides which may lead to reasonable adjustment by both sides. Under arbitration a mere compromise is expected and "the members on each side have to make out a case for their side. They do not come in the attitude that the other party may have something to say that is worth hearing."[1] State arbitration must therefore explicitly prove its superiority over conciliation; and similarly State regulation over collective bargaining, conciliation and arbitration itself. Finally, between the approach to State regulation seen in the Wages Councils and direct State legislation unassisted by the counsel of employers or workers, the latter must explicitly prove its superiority over the former. When left to Wages Councils the precise terms of the wages can be adjusted from time to time, or place to place; but written into the law of the land adjustment of terms is more

[1]*Dynamic Administration*, p. 235.

rigid, even though these terms may be left to departmental orders. Direct State regulation is thus more appropriate in implementing terms of employment likely to remain standard such as hours of labour and physical conditions. For instance, the last British consolidated Factory Act, that of 1937, dealt with cleanliness, overcrowding, air, light, safety, seats and weight lifting, and limited the hours of women and young persons to a nine-hour day and forty-eight-hour week.

Regulation by the State without participation of employers or workers is (assuming an efficient Civil Service) often more economical in time and effort than joint action and more stable through depression than employers' action. Nevertheless it is only resorted to as an implement for adjusting conditions of labour and terms of employment where special considerations apply. Six such considerations may be listed:

(i) Implementation by State regulation is the only possibility where the persons interested cannot judge their interests. Adult women though included with young persons under actual laws, need not be so regulated.

(ii) The State would benefit little by the advice of employers or workers on physical health when scientific research is of importance, rather than a balance of judgments.

(iii) If unofficial strikes against union-backed decisions and arbitration grow in number and severity, the ordinary collective bargaining between employers and workers may prove ineffective.

(iv) Collective bargaining without, or with insufficient, State participation may be considered to be pursuing aims contrary to the public interest. Trade union closed shop policies, for instance, may be thought a bar to mobility of labour, and the mere "participation" of the State not ample enough to avoid such policies.

(v) Collective bargaining with and without State participation is exercised industry by industry. Decisions, though to the interest of the several industries concerned, may not be in the interest of industry or the country as a whole. This point of view has become familiar in the demand for a national wages policy which only State regulation and control could achieve.

The demand is based on the need for labour mobility between industries. Left alone by the State, collective bargaining within each industry is likely to adjust wages and conditions to that of other industries so that work requiring equal skill and effort is equally paid in money and net advantages. Such "fair" wages will not result in movement in or out of the industry, and assume relatively static demand and supply conditions as between industries. If the products of one industry become more in demand (like munitions during a war, or houses or exports afterwards) there is no overall economic mechanism or organization to attract workers where they are needed, or to repel them by "unfair" wages where they are not needed.

(vi) Unemployment is caused mainly by national if not international circumstance, and a single industry is powerless to prevent unemployment by collective bargaining with or without State participation. Moreover different industries, as we have seen, suffer in very different degrees from unemployment. An industry of high unemployment risk could not by itself pay sufficient benefit to its unemployed. Palliative measures must be pooled nationally.

§5 PRINCIPLES OF JOINT CONTROL

The control of labour conditions in Britain and, indeed, most western democracies is obviously a complicated network of industrial relations. There is, however, a stout thread of logic running through the network which has been traced in the foregoing sections. Who the parties are that mainly exercise control depends on the terms or conditions of employment concerned, and the scope of the control. Table 18 sums up the existing situation in Britain by means of three columns for the main agencies of implementation and several rows for the main sorts of condition which can be controlled—policies can· thus be placed according to the policy-making agency and the conditions and terms of employment to which they refer. The several sorts of conditions correspond with those discussed in earlier chapters. The various methods of implementing policies distinguished in earlier sections of this chapter are reduced to three, as follows:

Column 1—Employers alone, §1.

TABLE 18: CHART OF THE CONTROL OVER TERMS OF EMPLOYMENT

Terms of Employment	POLICIES IMPLEMENTED BY:		
	(1) Employer alone	(2) Workers participation (Trade Union and Collective Bargaining)	(3) State participation and regulation
HOURS	Hours below Maximum Rest Pauses Speed of Work	Holidays with Pay Maxima for industries Overtime Pay Five-Day-Week	Maximum for all (Mines Acts, Shop Acts) Maximum for Women and Young Persons (Factory Acts)
TYPE AND METHOD OF WORK	Scientific Management Motion Study	Trade Practices Demarcation Rules Redeployment	
PHYSICAL CONDITIONS	Original Layout of Plant Technical Processes		Sanitary Code Safety Measures Poisonous Trades Regulation
SOCIAL RELATIONSHIPS	Welfare Work	Insurance Benefits	Social Insurance
AMOUNT OF WAGES	Rates above Basic Minima	Minimum Rates for Industries Grading Piece Lists	Wages Council (Trade Board) Minima for Industries
METHODS OF WAGES PAYMENT	Piece Rate Setting (Time Study)	Time or Piece Rates (and their relation)	No "truck"
SELECTION AND TRAINING OF INDIVIDUAL	"Hire and Fire" Personnel Dept.	"Closed Shop"	Technical Schooling Training Schemes Labour Exchange
SELECTION OF TYPES OF WORKER	"Dilution"	Ratio of Apprentices to Journeymen	Prohibition of Children's Employment

Column 2—Workers' and employers' collective bargaining, §2 and §3, i; State creation of bargaining bodies, §3, ii; State interposition in stages of negotiation (conciliation, mediation, arbitration), §3, iii.

Column 3—Full State participation in negotiation, §3, iv ; State regulation, §4.

The table exhibits certain gaps. Government departments have not up to the present had much to say about the type and method of work, or (except for prohibiting truck) about the methods of wage payment; nor have the workers had much to say about physical conditions, or (except for the closed shop) about the selection and training of individual persons. These gaps are significant of the underlying logic of the situation. The employer (whether capitalist or nationalized) is left to deal with details and methods, but the general results must accord with certain standards laid down either by collective bargaining with trade unions or else by the State. Which of these two methods of control predominates, depends largely on the degree of scientific knowledge that is applicable; the State can carry out conclusive research on physical conditions more readily than trade unions.

Standards are essentially negative; hours longer than forty-eight per week must not be worked by women, wages less than the minimum must not be paid. Hence the employer keeps the positive role in arranging the precise details. He usually proposes the precise hours and their arrangement (e.g., rest pauses), the precise wages to be paid above the basic minima and the precise individuals to be hired; and since the employer controls the technical details, the types of production, the layout of plant and the processes used, he is in a particularly advantageous position to determine the precise speed of work, and points of scientific management including motion study. In short, though the State and the workers share the principal responsibility for general standards and the State implements standards where scientific knowledge is applicable, the employer (whether capitalist, co-operative or nationalized) takes the initiative in detailed policy.

Nowhere is this role of the employer clearer than in the selection of individual workers. If demand for his products falls

H

off, it is he who must decide how many of his workers to lay off and thus initiate unemployment in various degrees. The modern employer working through his personnel department may be more humane or scientific than his predecessor who fired—as he hired—by rule of thumb; but his responsibility is nevertheless there. The State may palliate unemployment by benefits described in the next chapter, but can only prevent unemployment by acting as an employer or on employers. The State may take on workers itself, as for public works, or encourage private employers to do so, as by stimulating a more intensive investment policy.

Finally it must not be forgotten that in a free society the individual worker can still control the details of his life, as the individual employer controls the details of his business. Collective bargaining may fix a piece rate; but it is up to the individual worker, unless there is overwhelming pressure from his group, to earn as much as he likes by varying the number of pieces.

CHAPTER XIV

SOCIAL PROGRESS AND POLICY

§1 Criteria of Progress

BEFORE tracing how a society is progressing it is rational to set some objective or criterion, approach towards which shall constitute progress. What is the target at which we are aiming?

This is a work concerned mainly with fact and factual relations, not with aims or objectives. In assessing progress or suggesting the direction of policy, we can only take certain aims that seem generally agreed upon.[1] Many measures of progress agreed upon are clearly secondary. Efficiency, for instance, can be cited as a criterion only when the aim served is approved. An efficient burglar or an efficient dictator are worse socially than inefficient burglars or dictators, and increase in their number would hardly mark progress. Even industrial efficiency, the increased production per man-hour ("P.M.H.") and the reduction of costs, is important only in so far as it furthers some primary aim.

Among the agreed primary aims may be put health and wealth. The health of labour has been constantly referred to in past chapters, but depends on wider considerations than terms of employment, or unemployment. Wealth, or the conception of economic welfare, also has a wide scope. It is usually connected with the earning and the spending of the national dividend and brings human beings in as consumers as well as labourers and producers generally. Indeed, since producers are also consumers and the productive system presumably exists to produce goods directly or indirectly for consumption, the primary aim which economists tacitly or explicitly accept if they discuss policy or progress is usually the satisfaction of the consumer. But they are not always explicit as to whether it is the consumer's demands, his wants, or his needs that are

[1]*See* Florence, *Uplift in Economics* (American edition, *Sociology and Sin*) for the relation of Social Science to policy.

to be satisfied. The demand which economists claim to measure
or at least to estimate consists in wants that the consumer is
willing and able to pay for out of income at a specific demand
price. A consumer with a large income can demand a luxurious
want at a higher price than a poor consumer can a want
necessary for his health, so that with unequal distribution of
income, demands are by no means identical with wants, much
less with needs. Needs in the sense of what is necessary for
health or more generally what is "good" for people is not
necessarily what consumers will want of their own volition, and
is still further removed from demand.

What is "good for people" is not, however, agreed upon,
and economists must fall back largely on the satisfaction of
wants as a criterion. If income were evenly distributed and
stable, this would not deviate greatly from satisfaction of
demand. The target accepted by economists has been stated
most explicitly perhaps by Professor Pigou in his *Wealth and
Welfare*,[1] as an increasing, stable, and evenly-distributed
national real income. The use of real is explained later.[2] With
the modern fashion for alphabetical abbreviation this aim may
be referred to as ISENRI. From the standpoint of individual
happiness it is increasing income per head of population that is
important rather than the aggregate national income and the
aim may be amended by adding *per person*. The adjective
national is retained, to indicate that it is not merely private
incomes per person that are referred to. The abbreviation now
becomes ISENRIP.

Health and wealth, particularly in their more measurable
forms, appear to many people as too grossly materialistic.
There is, they contend, mental as well as physical health, and
riches that are not material riches. Leaving aside for the present
the question how far mental health does not largely depend on
physical health, and a rich and varied life on material riches,
we must strive to discover and define agreed-upon non-material
and non-economic criteria of progress.

In a manual on labour it must certainly be stressed that
there are values connected with work apart from the economic

[1]The original edition of *Economics of Welfare*.
[2]Table 20, and p. 209.

value of the output in consumption. There is interest in the work depending largely on type of worker and type of work. Modern regional surveys, for instance, put forward one aim in planning as the assurance of a choice of type of work in any locality, so that different types of temperament and ability may find their level.[1] Modern industrial tendencies, such as localization of trades and large factories and firms, threaten democracy as well as variety in choice of work. Many hold the view that if an industrial reform can be achieved either way, it is better to do it democratically through, say, trade unions, than paternalistically through a benevolent State Government. Interest in work and the democratic control of working conditions, though industrial, are not materialistic, and as tests for general social progress link up with non-material criteria not related to industry. Such general criteria that are measurable include the proportion of persons being educated (or on the other hand illiterate) among the population; the hours spent in various uses of leisure (partly dependent on hours and fatigue of work); expenditure on (and number of clients of) various social services. Many criteria more or less commonly agreed upon are less capable of measurement. Among these two have come into prominence with the modern enthusiasm for town and country planning, namely, community spirit and amenity. Community spirit is as yet insufficiently agreed upon, or measurable, to serve as a useful criterion, but amenity is referred to so often that it should be at least roughly defined and further considered.

In the survey for the planning of Worcester,[2] amenities were first distinguished from services (such as medical treatment or education) offered to *individual* cases and groups, as services offered to the general public. They were further distinguished from public utilities, as contributing to the recreation and culture of the general public, rather than to their physical health and prosperity. Amenities in short are not necessaries to health or economic efficiency, but something free to the general public

[1] e.g., Glaisyer, Brennan, Ritchie and Florence, *County Town*, pp. 42, 73-76, 88.
[2] Glaisyer, Brennan, Ritchie and Florence, *County Town*, pp. 174, 180.

over and above that. Examples that occur and recur in plans for towns are the *general* lay-out, for instance at Worcester a wide river embankment and opening up of vistas upon the cathedral and city churches;[1] and *specific* amenities like parks, swimming baths and concerts. Specific amenities thus serve as facilities for the use of leisure and their development might be measured either by expenditure incurred or by the number of persons actually using them.

To test for progress, the actual situation to-day and the actual course of events during the last hundred years will now be set against those criteria. The adjective actual is stressed because many people are influenced by speculations and prognostications not supported by the exact observation of current facts.

As far as labour is concerned, the predictions of Karl Marx have a great vogue. They were certainly based on observations of the facts some hundred years ago by Marx himself, but his followers have been slow in carrying out Marx's own methods. They have mostly been content to repeat his views, raising them to the level of dogmas from which deductions are made, rather than to check his conclusions by independent induction from new facts—and, of course, the facts now recorded are more comprehensive and more exactly measured than ever were those that Marx was able to quote. Marx foresaw as a result of the historical tendency of capitalist accumulation the growth of the "mass of misery, oppression, slavery, degradation, exploitation."[2] To quote a particular instance, he thought the extensive introduction of female and child labour would be necessary to counterbalance the assumed tendency for a falling rate of profit.[3] This misery was certainly present in England in Marx's day. But have the living and working conditions of labour, in fact, got worse? Without worrying about the philosophy of history and immanent laws of capitalistic production that are supposed to act with the "inexorability of a law of Nature" we will turn to what has actually happened in recent history.

[1] op cit., pp. 180, 181.
[2] *Das Kapital*, Vol. I, Chap. XXXII.
[3] op. cit., Vol. III, Chap. XIV.

§2 THE ACTUAL COURSE OF PROGRESS

Looking back a hundred years there is little question that Britain has progressed, judged by the physical, economic or other criteria proposed. Physical health can be measured by death rates and infant mortality. The trend of both since 1870 is given in Table 19. Death rates show an almost continuous

TABLE 19: BIRTH AND DEATH RATES, GREAT BRITAIN AND NORTHERN IRELAND 1870-1945[1]

Year	Birth Rates (Crude per 1,000 population)	Death Rates per 1,000 population		Infant Mortality Deaths in First Year, per 1,000 born
		Males	Females	
1870-2	35.0	23.3	20.8	150
1880-2	33.7	20.8	18.6	137
1890-2	30.6	20.7	18.6	145
1900-2	28.6	18.4	16.3	142
1910-2	24.6	14.9	13.3	110
1920-2	23.1	13.5	11.9	82
1930-2	16.3	12.9	11.5	67
1935	15.2	12.7	11.3	60
1940	14.6	16.2	13.0	60
1945	16.2	14.9	11.0	49

fall till in 1945 they were nearly half the 1870-2 rate—a fall too large to be attributed merely to the change in the age structure. Infant mortality shows a still more remarkable fall to about one-third of the rate in 1870-2. The tests of economic progress included in ISENRIP (increasing, stable and evenly-distributed real income per person) can be combined by tracing the economic position of the poorer sections of the community, that is, of labour living by wages, rather than salaries, rent, interest or profit. The rich have had a comfortable margin between their actual income and the expenditure necessary to ward off starvation or near starvation, and it is only among the poor that health, comfort and efficiency has been likely to

[1]Source—Annual Abstract of Statistics 1935-46, pp. 17, 23, 28.

suffer by a decline or fluctuation in income. If the lot of the wage-earning class is improving and improving steadily most of the economic tests proposed will be satisfied. Three measures of the changing lot of labour will be described: the trend in the proportion in primary poverty, the trend of real wages of those employed and (to test regularity of income over time) changes in the purchasing power of the working population employed or unemployed.

In England to-day fewer workers than in the days of sweated labour earn, when in full employment, less than subsistence, i.e., the minimum needed for their own health and efficiency, together with that of their dependants.[1] A series of local social surveys beginning with Charles Booth's *Life and Labour of the People of London*, published in 1889, and Seebohm Rowntree's *Poverty* (a study of York), published in 1901 have ascertained the income of working-class families (usually including an adult male breadwinner and one other earner) and calculated the expenditure necessary for their subsistence. Comparing actual income and necessary expenditure family by family these surveys arrive at the proportion of working-class families below the poverty line. This line of "primary" poverty varies, of course, with the size of the family, but assumes that families spend their money to the best advantage for health and efficiency.

Two of these surveys were repeated and the proportion of working-class families in poverty compared for the different dates by the same standard. Investigating five medium-sized towns (Reading, Northampton, Bolton, Warrington, and Stanley in County Durham), Professor Bowley and his assistants found that if full-time wages were assumed received in both years, the proportion of families below the bare subsistence level in the five towns fell from 11 to 4 per cent between 1913 and 1924. Repeating his survey at York in 1936 Seebohm Rowntree found that, in spite of a higher unemployment rate, the percentage of all families which were below bare subsistence level had fallen from 15·5 to 6·8 per cent. Among all families, the income was insufficient because of low wages in 8.0 per cent of cases in 1899, but only 0.6 per cent in 1936.

[1] See above, Chapter VII, §1, for method of calculating the minimum.

The increased value of average earnings, in terms of the conditions for health and working capacity, is confirmed by the trend of "real" wages calculated by comparing changes in wages with changes in the cost of living. Changes in the cost of living are measured by index numbers, giving the percentages by which the prices of a standard set of representative articles have varied from a given base period. Until 1947 the Ministry of Labour's cost of living index used a budget in which the main classes of expenditure were weighted as in the first column of Table 12.[1]

Changes in the wage rates of given occupations and grades (and consequently, if hours and speed of work remain unchanged, in earnings too) can be measured like the cost of living by index numbers which pick out the rates of a standard set of occupations as representative of the work of the bulk of the working population. The index which goes back farthest is that devised by Professor Bowley[2] and this index of wages is put side by side with the official index of the cost of living in Table 20, each with the same base year of 1924. Dividing the wage index by the cost of living index the last column of the table gives the changes in "real" wages, i.e., the living conditions money wages can purchase. Though war-time changes and

TABLE 20: CALCULATION OF CHANGES IN REAL WAGES, 1924-45

Year	Changes in Cost of Living. Ministry of Labour Index	Changes in Wage Rates, Bowley's Index	Changes in Real Wages
	per cent	per cent	per cent
1924	100	100	100
1929	94	$99\frac{1}{4}$	$105\frac{1}{2}$
1933	$79\frac{1}{2}$	94	118
1936	84	$97\frac{1}{2}$	116
1939	91	$105\frac{3}{4}$	116
1945	116	$160\frac{3}{4}$	$138\frac{1}{2}$

[1]For the choice of weighting of each article of consumption within the main classes, see Ministry of Labour Gazette.

[2]For the details of its composition, see London and Cambridge Economic Service Bulletins.

H*

rationing in particular make a fixed budget of goods and services rather an unreal basis for any exact cost of living calculation, the purchasing power of wages over the necessaries of life for health and efficiency[1] appear to have been rising between 1924 and 1945 by 38 per cent. Before the war, between 1924 and 1939, they had risen by 16 per cent.

There is a further point on the distribution of incomes. Not only are the real wages of wage-earners rising and the proportion in poverty falling, but there has been a certain up-grading of wage-earners into the salaried class. The British Census of Production is definite on this point. In 1924 there were 15·6 per cent in the administrative, technical and clerical staff of productive establishment to every hundred operatives; by 1930 the proportion was 17·6 per cent, and by 1935 19·6 per cent. This up-grading is confirmed by the conclusion[2] of Colin Clark as to the "most striking growth in the salariat. The numbers of well-paid salary-earners have increased nearly threefold since 1911 (up to 1929-32), and their share of the national income has risen from 7 to 13-15 per cent." This increase is partly accounted for by the displacement of independent employers, but by no means entirely.

So far, a rising trend in the incomes of labour has been established. Unemployment, however, was greater between 1920 and 1938 than before 1914 and this suggests that in years of extreme unemployment such as 1931-4 the real income or purchasing power of labour must have fallen heavily, and that labour's real income, though increasing generally and more evenly distributed, has become liable to greater irregularity. To test this I calculated the changes during the slump phase of the trade cycle of 1929-35 in the money wages of insured workers still in employment, together with the insurance benefit of those unemployed, and corrected for changes in the cost of living. The unexpected result[3] was "the maintenance and

[1] The budget of goods and services is in theory an average budget for the working class as a whole, not a minimum for cost of subsistence. In fact, however, the basic budget, collected in 1904, overweights food and is more like a real cost of living budget than an average for goods and services bought in 1946.

[2] Colin Clark, *National Income and Outlay* (1937), p. 100.

[3] *Journal of Political Economy*, October 1936.

surpassing of the 1929 working class purchasing-power level in every year through the period of depression. This remains true even when population growth is taken into account and purchasing-power is reckoned per head. . . . These results were primarily due to a fall in the cost of living which far outstripped the fall in wages, but the influence of the payments (of benefit) to the unemployed must not be neglected." Falls in prices normally accompany depressions and this factor offsetting unemployment is usually present; but the off-setting may not be complete, and will, in any case, not compensate the unemployed for the difference between their former wages and present benefits. What happens to real income in a depression is that there is an uneven distribution as between workers. Those remaining in full employment are better off owing to a fall in the cost of living, the unemployed, in spite of this fall, considerably poorer, unless benefits are exceptionally generous.

By the economic test, then, of increasing stable and evenly-distributed real income per head, the last fifty years (in spite of devastating wars and a continuing though slowing-down increase of population and considerable unemployment) have not been leading to mass misery—obviously rather the contrary.

In a manual on labour the non-economic tests of progress do not require lengthy discussion. It is sufficient to point to the steady reduction of hours of labour from the ten or more, six days a week, worked even by women and children eighty to a hundred years ago, as quoted from official sources by Marx,[1] to the present normal practice of a five-and-a-half- or five-day week of eight to nine hours per day, and the exclusion from industry altogether of children under fifteen; to point to the growth in the proportion of wage earners' children at school and university from practically nil a hundred years ago to all up to age fifteen and many scholars after that; and to point to the growth in membership and power of the trade unions and "industrial democracy" described in the previous chapter.

Whether interest in work has progressed is, however, held in doubt. Many writers conclude that there is more boredom and monotony in industry and less craftsmanship than heretofore. The discussion in chapters IV, V and IX showed that the

[1]*Das Kapital*, Volume I, Chapter X.

issue is by no means simple, since boredom is a state of mind due to a relation of worker and work and not inherent in type of work alone. It is true that technological advance has made work to-day more specialized, but this may relieve the workers prone to boredom from many boring "chores" incidental to all-round jobs. The changing structure of industry must also be recalled. More people are now engaged in administration, transport and services which the average person appears to find interesting as being more companionable; fewer are engaged in physically strenuous labour.

As for progress in amenity, the salient point is that the very technological advance to which so much social progress is attributed has been an enemy. Though the prosperity of the modern towns and "conurbations" of England has depended on industrial development, their amenity has suffered from smoke and the other neighbourhood nuisances[1] of factories, railways and mines and the refuse and "Black Country" left behind. To be sure many towns have laid out parks and boulevards in their outer fringes and suburbs, yet it is doubtful whether these have compensated for the growing spread of urban conditions into the countryside and for the increasing congestion of traffic. The balance may, however, be redressed in the future by the new interest in physical planning, particularly in its advocacy of redeveloped city centres, and of zoning of factories. Labour, whose homes have in the past usually been crowded next the factories, and who found no refreshment in any graciousness of shopping and social centre may at length regain the amenity lost by industrialism.

§3 The Causes and Future of Progress

So much for certain trends towards progress in the past. The question that must now be asked is, will they continue and how far can they continue in the future? The answer lies in tracing the causes and the inter-relationship of these separate trends, incidentally pointing to "records" actually achieved elsewhere than in Britain.

Certain inter-relations are fairly obvious. A greater national

---

[1]For an analysis of nuisances see Glaisyer, Brennan, Ritchie and Florence, *County Town*, Chapter IV, Table XIII.

income more evenly distributed allows fewer hours to be worked even if this means a lower output (which, within limits, it usually does not). Shorter hours mean greater leisure and less fatigue, if there is not longer travel to work or more speeding up at work. More leisure and less fatigue probably mean a greater demand for education and amenity. Certainly the high national real income per head in the United States is associated with a high proportion of university students. While in 1932 in England and Wales only about two out of a hundred aged twenty to twenty-three were at a university and the number remained much the same till the outbreak of war; in the United States the proportion was eleven per hundred and was rising. Thus, social progress is not just an advance along a few isolated measurable lines but is an integrated whole forming a sort of virtuous circle. Material advance goes hand-in-hand with non-material. Neither of them necessarily comes first. If recreation and educational activities are rendered possible by higher real wages and shorter hours of work, it may also be true that it was their members' desire for more education and recreation, which lay behind trade union demands and which forced employers to grant wage concessions, the five-day week and holidays with pay.

This close relationship between the various indices of progress makes it easier to trace a few fundamental causes at work. First, I should put technical inventions, here (though not always elsewhere) finding contact with the Marxian thesis. The Marxian interpretation of history, often called economic, is also a technological interpretation claiming in an oft-quoted passage that[1] "in acquiring new productive forces men change their mode of production; and in changing their mode of production they change their way of earning their living—they change all their social relations. The hand-mill gives you society with the feudal lord, the steam-mill society with the industrial capitalist." Certainly, modern economic organization and modes of production have been revolutionized by the productive forces unleashed by scientific invention. Larger factories and firms, able to use more powerful and more specialized equip-

[1]Marx, "The Poverty of Philosophy" (*A Handbook of Marxism*, p. 355).

ment[1] and (thanks to mechanized transport) able to localize far from material and markets have produced the existing wants of mankind at less cost, not only in money but in muscle and fatigue; and new inventions meet consumers' new wants. There is no sign that scientific invention is flagging and, provided that its destructive uses are kept in check, and (as we shall argue later) that sufficient adaptability to its requirements exists in social and political organization, there is no reason to foresee a check in progress generally. Wars and their aftermath have slowed and are slowing down progress (particularly total real income) in certain countries, not excepting England, but if there are no further world wars and society can reorganize to avoid the problems such as unemployment partly caused by rapid technical advance itself, then that advance should spell a continuance if not an acceleration of the social progress of the last hundred years.

A fundamental cause at work only second to technological advance is in Western civilization the fall in the birth rate. The reduction in the number of families and persons in primary poverty in England between 1900, 1911, 1924 and 1935 traced in the surveys of Bowley and Rowntree was in part attributed by them, as we have seen, to a decrease in the typical size of families. Similar social surveys made in 1937 and 1938 in places where unemployment was low, showed large families to be almost the only cause of primary poverty. The fall in the birth rate acts in co-operation with technical advance to ensure progress, if by progress we continue to mean not the aggregate income of the country but the average per head. In countries like India or Egypt wherever technical improvements such as dams for irrigation and railways have been introduced, the increased and better distributed food supplies have lowered death rates. With no fall in birth rates, population has in consequence increased. Between 1930 and 1940 India, for instance, increased her population by fifty million. There is little sign, however, that the poorer members of the population of these countries are fewer or less in poverty. Is a mere increase in population progress?

The same fast increase in population occurred in Britain

[1]See Florence, *Investment, Location and Size of Plant.*

up to 1876-80 when the birth rate was still 35·3 and was only just beginning to fall. In spite of emigration and a peaceful technical advance hardly likely to be equalled (since England was then specializing for a world market), the mass of poverty was only slowly diminishing. Malthus writing in 1798-1803 gave an actually (and not merely theoretically) correct account of the facts for his time and place; his account still remains correct for most of the world's people. Population tends to outrun the means of subsistence and if there are no preventive checks, the positive checks indicated by high death rates must eventually "repress the superior power of population and keep its effects on a level with the means of subsistence."[1]

Just as technical invention has a "snag" that it may be used in war to destroy the world, so the fall in the birth-rate may also proceed too far. Once started there is a snowball effect. If births from the year x to the year y fall by, say, half there are in the year $y+20$ likely to be only half the number of women of twenty and (if fertility rates remain the same) to be only half the number of births from that age group as in the year y. The year $y+40$ will by the same logic have the likelihood of only about a quarter of the births from women aged twenty as in the year x. Estimates of the population of Great Britain forecast a slow fall of about one million from 1950 to 1960 and a faster rate of fall of about two million from 1960 to 1970.[2]

§4 PROGRESS AND SOCIAL POLICY

A third fundamental factor in social progress is formed by deliberate social policy. In the Victorian era this was often called the growth of a social conscience; but now policy is largely the result of democratic power—government of the people for the people—not by a benevolent governing class but —by the people. Many organizations besides democratic national and local governments have by their policy been advancing social progress. In the past, voluntary private societies have often been the pioneers in social work; and democratically organized trade unions were (as described in the last chapter) the chief agency in increasing wage rates and

[1]*Essay on Population* (1803), Chapter XI.
[2]Enid Charles in *Political Arithmetic* (ed. Hogben), pp. 73-105.

reducing hours of labour. In raising real wages by lowering prices the consumers' co-operative movement has contributed by its policy of a dividend on purchase rather than on privately-owned capital.

These policies are largely concerned with regularizing and evenly distributing the national income rather than increasing its total. The neglect of total income may indeed prove a snag in democratic policy comparable with the snags in technical progress and falling birth rates. Neglect rests on the assumption among wage earners that their share of total income has little connection with their own output and efficiency, but can always be made up by transference of wealth from richer classes. This assumption not so wide of the facts in nineteenth-century Britain will no doubt receive a shock from the logic of events in twentieth-century Britain after two world wars; but how rude the shock and how adjustable ruling ideas after the shock largely depends, as will be illustrated, on the spread of economic and political science.

Meanwhile social policy is greatly concerned with distributing and evening out income by palliatives. It has attempted to prevent such occurrences as unemployment, low wages, accidents, illness, death, but failing that, to palliate their consequences. Thus a factory safety code enforced by Government inspectors tries to reduce industrial accidents, but if an accident does occur, compensation must by law be paid to the injured worker to make up (or partly make up) for his loss of earnings and his medical treatment.

Preventive measures against inefficiency in employment (and their degree of success) have already been described in Part II; and against unemployment in Part III. In this section the great part policy has played in social progress must be rounded out by a review of palliative measures. Their growing magnitude can be judged from the fact that between 1913-4 and 1933-4 the money paid out in poor relief, in widows and old age pensions, and in health and unemployment benefit rose from £41,500,000 to £248,000,000, or clear of workers' contributions from about £32,000,000 to £200,000,000. Correcting for a contemporaneous rise in the cost of living of 41 per cent this amounts to roughly a four to fivefold rise in the real expenditure, used mainly for evening out the unequal distribution of wealth.

The bulk of palliatives are now included in the term social security. For the events against which palliatives are sought can be looked upon as risks or emergencies against which labour desires to be secured. The risks may either be connected with the life cycle of all "from the womb to the tomb," or specifically to employment, or neither. Take the emergencies of life, age by age. There is maternity benefit for mothers, family allowances for children and pensions for orphans and their widowed mothers at one end of the age scale; at the other, pensions for women aged sixty and men aged sixty-five, and funeral benefit. These payments made automatically at certain ages are rational, since as all social surveys have found, families tend to sink below the poverty line during the period of reproduction and while the children are still dependent, and later when the original couple reaches old age. Employment and other risks on the other hand are only partly dependent on age. Employment risks include occupational diseases, injury by industrial accident, and unemployment; other risks, sickness, disability and death from war and general non-industrial causes. At first, palliative measures against these different types of risks were organized somewhat differently in separate schemes nationally or otherwise; but following on the Beveridge Report of 1944, more uniformity in conditions and in the scale of contributions (if any) and of benefits is being introduced, largely by the extension of national insurance to cover all persons.

From the standpoint of efficiency and progress the main question is whether these palliative measures encourage or possibly stand in the way of the more important preventive measures. Prevention may be better than cure, but both prevention and cure are better than palliatives. To take two instances; does the system of compensation for accidents give the employers an incentive to prevent accidents? And will unemployment benefits give the workers with families any incentive to seek work? In England up to the present an employer can insure against accidents to his employees with a private assurance company and this company, though it has different premium rates for different industries and occupations, may or may not adjust his premium according to the risk in the employer's own factory. If premium rates are not adjusted (as they are in several American states) according to the employer's accident experience or to inspectors' assessments, then the employer has less financial incentive than otherwise to prevent accidents. Again, if the unemployed get an allowance for children while the employed do not (as was the situation in England from 1912 to 1947), it may pay paterfamilias with many children to stay out of work. Even under the present arrangement the unemployed get benefit for the first child, the employed do not. An employed man often has to spend money on travel, working clothes and contributions which an unemployed man does not have to spend; so that the gap between the advantage of work elsewhere and in some other trade, and of staying unemployed may be dangerously narrow. Palliatives if they check mobility of labour, will hardly be helping to prevent or even to cure unemployment.

§5 Policy Enlightened and Informed

The development of a social policy that has helped to raise the mode of life and status of labour has not just been the result of bourgeois goodwill and labour power. The discoveries of natural science laid the foundation for our present material progress; discovery in human and biological sciences has been helping the distribution of the results of that progress, and initiating a wider advance. Biology contributed towards the preventive measures against sickness causing absences from industry, and toward public health generally. The fall in death rates has been largely due to reduced deaths from diseases of which we now know the causes, though we did not a hundred years ago. The fall has been particularly marked among the poorer sections of the community and has thus levelled down the class differences in death rates.

Similar progress in the future may be helped on by developments in economic science. Here the avoidance of unemployment without prejudice to efficient production and incentives to labour may be a test case, and has already been discussed. Social progress in the long run requires, however, more than enlightenment on economics. The question who is, in fact, in control of employment and labour policy was dealt with in earlier chapters and clearly more enlightenment is needed on the wider questions of political science. Direct control of policies affecting general social progress is, in modern Britain, in the hands of private business firms, co-operative societies or local or central Government; indirect control in the hands of trade unions. Much more scientific information is needed on the relative capacities of these agencies of control and their methods of management, if economic and democratic objectives and even a life of greater amenity are to be efficiently approached.

The labour movement has so long fought through trade unions for its share of profits or through co-operative societies for the elimination of profits that it has neglected the importance of reducing costs; yet reduction in prices and hence a higher real income for labour can probably go further by attention to cost than to profits. In retailing, for instance, the average net profit margin (balancing out the losses and gains of individual firms) is probably between 2 to 5 per cent of the retail price,[1] but average retailing cost margins added to the wholesaler's price are of the order of 15 to 30 per cent of retail prices. Costs can probably be heavily reduced by changes in organization if a scientific study is made of the elements of organization. These elements include the size of the whole organization, and within the organization, the methods of appointment and dismissal, the methods of division of labour (such as functional specialization) in manual work and management, and the manageable size and number of constituent departments and sub-departments. Management itself is capable of scientific study, and we have examined how far each of the different agencies of control—the employer, the trade unions and the State—has succeeded in implementing this science which includes industrial psychology and "personnel" management.

Trade unions, and as employers, the co-operative move-

---

[1]There is still no Census of Distribution in Britain, but the *U.S. Census of Distribution* of 1929 estimated the overall retail profit margins as less than 2 per cent. The overall retail costs margin, excluding interest on capital, was 25 per cent.

ment and the local authorities are certainly firmly based on democratic control; but here again there seems to be a snag in that they appear lacking in knowledge of the methods of management and organization, in the adaptability, enterprise and perhaps imagination needed for cost reduction and progress in a changing world. Obstacles to social progress which they have fought and largely overcome in the past, were so obvious that little imagination was required; they have secured sanitary and well-policed communities, minimum living wages and "human" hours as a maximum, and some reduction of prices that exploited the consumer; yet more remains to be done. It is possible to reduce prices still further by more efficient organization that will cut down costs themselves, to initiate research and exploit new inventions, and (if a fuller life is to be attainable by everyone) to provide a variety of amenities for leisure hours and for income surplus to needs. Signs are not lacking that the particular form and methods of management and organization of these democratic bodies may be holding up progress. There is too direct and short-sighted an application of so-called democratic principles such as promotion by seniority in the service, regardless of capacity and education. Few, if any, can come on to the administrative staff of a retail and wholesale co-operative society, trade union or even a local authority who have not left school at sixteen and thus missed higher schooling and the university altogether. The theory is that it would not be fair on those climbing the ladder from the age of fourteen or sixteen if graduates in their twenties, however well selected, educated, and trained were let in on a higher rung. This theory may not have stood in the way of the efficient use of capacities fifty years ago, when many capable boys and girls missed through poverty any chance of reaching higher schooling or the university. But with the thorough scholarship system now being developed for the more intelligent children, the co-operative movement will be choosing at fifteen and sixteen its future managers, and trade unions and local government authorities their officers, from those graded too low in the scale of intelligence to get scholarships. Unless soon remedied this staffing practice will presumably give the balance of advantages in progressive efficiency to the alternative organizations of the central State and private capitalist business, in spite of their countervailing disadvantages.

Discussing the prevention of unemployment, a policy of progressive investment in capital equipment was contrasted with a cautious preference for liquid assets which restricts expansion of employment. Consumers' co-operation has played a great part in keeping down the cost of living, and presents great possibilities in the cheap provision of capital. Yet evidence is to hand that the wholesale co-operative societies of Britain, manufacturers of a wide variety of goods staffed almost entirely by up-grading procedure, adopt this cautious, unprogressive policy, keeping a much higher proportion of their assets liquid than the average capitalist company.[1] Here, in fact, may be a significant example of a difference in policy due to a difference in the type of entrepreneur. Where the key men are paid by salary like co-operative directors or managers, the incentive to invest progressively may well fall off. For while failure of the investment may bring disgrace, success brings no additional personal gain.

Risk of increasing losses from overhead costs if the market is not anticipated correctly, may be slowing down investment in equipment and may have accounted for the inter-war increase in hard core unemployment. Even if large organization takes the place of many smaller firms and thus reduces the uncertainties of competition, these large organizations, whether co-operative societies, joint stock companies or trade associations offer incentives (such as salaries) weaker than profits to the key man in control of investment policy. Moreover, if these organizations are large in relation to the whole industry, they may be virtual monopolies permitting profitable restrictions of output.

The key to social progress—the avoidance of unemployment and rising productivity per man and hence rising standards of living and amenities—lies today largely with the top management of big industrial enterprises whether co-operative or nationalized or controlled by capital. It is a problem in practical political science to find the staffing procedure which will bring

[1]Carr-Saunders, Florence and Peers, *Consumers' Co-operation in Great Britain* (Second Edition,) Chapter XXV.

the more efficient and enterprising managers to the top. Yet so far from remedies being sought the problem in political science is often not recognized. May this manual contribute towards greater understanding of the human and social sources of labour efficiency and progress.

END

LIST OF BOOKS FOR FURTHER READING

I. OFFICIAL DOCUMENTS AND CURRENT PERIODICALS.

Industrial Health (formerly Fatigue) Research Board; Reports referred to in text Nos. 19, 21, 24, 37, 39, 51, 54, 55, 59, 62, 68, 69, 75, 76, 84, 86, 88, 90; Emergency Report 1; 18th Annual Report.

Industrial Relations Handbook. Ministry of Labour.

Labour Gazette (monthly). Ministry of Labour.

Occupational Psychology (formerly the *Human Factor*). National Institute of Industrial Psychology.

Public Health Bulletin 106. U.S. Public Health Service.

II. GENERAL REFERENCE TO LABOUR.

G. D. H. Cole. *Organized Labour*. Allen & Unwin, 1924.

Z. C. Dickinson. *Compensating Industrial Effort*. Ronald Press, 1937.

M. Dobb. *Wages*. Cambridge Press & Nisbet, (Revised) 1946.

P. S. Florence. *Economics of Fatigue and Unrest*. Allen & Unwin, 1924.

F. J. Roethlisberger and W. J. Dickson. *Management and the Worker*. Harvard Press, 1939.

H. M. Vernon. *Industrial Fatigue and Efficiency*. Routledge, 1923.

S. and B. Webb. *Industrial Democracy*. Longman's (Revised), 1911.

III. SPECIFIC REFERENCE TO THE THEORY OF EMPLOYMENT.

W. Beveridge. *Full Employment in a Free Society*. Allen & Unwin, 1944.

E. H. Chamberlin. *The Theory of Monopolistic Competition*. Harvard University Press, 1946.

A. Hansen. *Full Recovery and Stagnation*. A. and C. Black, 1938.

J. M. Keynes. *General Theory of Employment, Interest and Money.* Macmillan & Co., 1936.
J. Meade. *Economic Analysis and Policy.* Clarendon Press, 1937.
Joan Robinson. *Economics of Imperfect Competition.* Macmillan & Co., 1933.
Joan Robinson. *Introduction to the Theory of Employment.* Macmillan & Co., 1937.

IV. BACKGROUND OF INDUSTRIAL ORGANIZATION AND SOCIAL INSTITUTIONS.
Planning Surveys, e.g., Glaisyer *et al. County Town.* John Murray, 1947.
Social Surveys, e.g., Rowntree. *Poverty and Progress.* Longman's, 1941.
P. S. Florence. *The Logic of Industrial Organization.* Kegan Paul, 1933.
J. H. Richardson. *Industrial Relations in Great Britain.* I.L.O. and Allen & Unwin, 1938.
F. W. Taylor. *Principles of Scientific Management.* Harpers, (First Edition), 1911.
O. Tead and H. C. Metcalfe. *Personnel Administration.* McGraw Hill Co. (Third Edition), 1933.

INDEX

E

G

H

INDEX

For Product Safety Concerns and Information please contact our EU
representative GPSR@taylorandfrancis.com Taylor & Francis Verlag GmbH,
Kaufingerstraße 24, 80331 München, Germany

Printed and bound by CPI Group (UK) Ltd, Croydon, CR0 4YY
08/05/2025
01864470-0001